CHINA'S
HIDDEN
CHILDREN

CHINA'S
HIDDEN
CHILDREN

*Abandonment, Adoption, and the Human
Costs of the One-Child Policy*

KAY ANN JOHNSON

The University of Chicago Press | *Chicago and London*

The University of Chicago Press, Chicago 60637
The University of Chicago Press, Ltd., London
© 2016 by The University of Chicago
All rights reserved. Published 2016.
Paperback edition 2017
Printed in the United States of America

23 22 21 20 19 18 17   4 5 6 7 8

ISBN-13: 978-0-226-35251-0 (cloth)
ISBN-13: 978-0-226-52907-3 (paper)
ISBN-13: 978-0-226-35265-7 (e-book)
DOI: 10.7208/chicago/9780226352657.001.0001

Library of Congress Cataloging-in-Publication Data

Johnson, Kay Ann, author.
China's hidden children : abandonment, adoption, and the human costs of the
one-child policy / Kay Ann Johnson.
pages ; cm
Includes bibliographical references and index.
ISBN 978-0-226-35251-0 (cloth : alk. paper) — ISBN 978-0-226-35265-7
(e-book) 1. Abandoned children—China. 2. Girls—Civil rights—China.
3. Intercountry adoption—China. 4. Child trafficking—China. 5. China—
Population policy—Social aspects. 6. Family size—Government policy—Social
aspects—China. I. Title.
HV887.C6J66 2016
362.70951—dc23
2015028490

TO WANG LIYAO (1940–2013), my colleague, close friend, and research partner for most of the work that appears in this book. His wisdom, kindness, and generosity inspired this project and shaped the understanding it conveys. Following his wishes, the research presented here is further dedicated to the hundreds of people who have shared their personal stories with us and, above all, to the 120,000 children who were sent out of China in the wake of the one-child policy and their current and former families.

CONTENTS

PREFACE

The initial impetus to turn my attention as a China scholar to the investigation of infant abandonment, its causes, and consequences arose from my own adoption of a three-month-old foundling in March 1991. I did not know at that time that my daughter would be one of the first of over 120,000 children to leave China through international adoption over the next twenty years, 85,000 of them to the United States. Adopting just at the beginning of this exodus, I spent five weeks visiting a large state orphanage that was beginning to sink into crisis due to underfunding in the face of escalating numbers of infants arriving at the orphanage.[1] Like most adoptive parents, I wondered about the people who gave birth to my daughter and apparently left her on the streets of a big city. Ever since that time, I have pursued this study as both a China scholar and an adoptive mother of a child who was born and abandoned in the midst of what I later learned was one of the largest, most brutal birth planning campaigns that ever swept the rural areas of central south China.[2]

I hoped that through my research I could provide for my daughter a record of what was happening at the time she was abandoned, a record that could foster some understanding about her origins by placing them in their historical, political, economic, and social context. Such understanding, I imagined, could help mitigate feelings of bitterness against her birth parents and, above all, help assuage a young child's often unspoken worries about "what was wrong with me," "what did I do wrong to lose my parents," worries my daughter articulated when she was only three years old. Placing her personal abandonment story in the larger historical context of this era might help depersonalize what happened to her and connect her to a larger cohort of girls who also lost their original families, many of whom were sent into international adoption, although I soon learned that most remained in China as daughters in adoptive Chinese families, one of the most important findings of our research.

Ultimately, the issue of origins is only one of many that adoptees might grapple with. Now as the mother of a twenty-something daughter from China, it is clear to me that issues of identity among young adult adoptees growing up in the United States are rooted in the country and society where they have been raised. They live as a minority of a minority in a race-conscious society that constructs family and kinship ideals around biological connections. However, an important feature of the racial constructions that children adopted from China grow up with in the United States is an image of China as a place that does not value daughters, where girls are seen as "the maggots in the rice" and "goods on which one loses,"[3] so much so that girl babies are "dumped on the streets like kittens in a sack," as it was put by the British filmmaker of *The Dying Rooms*, a documentary on Chinese orphanages widely publicized in the mid-1990s and well known in the China adoption community.[4] These are the images that many adoptees grow up with in the United States, images that greatly distort the views and experiences of the rural parents we met who relinquished their daughters under circumstances that are little understood in the United States. Even the term "abandonment," a legal category for the purpose of regulating adoption as well as a description of an act of desertion, often obscures more than it reveals about why and how a child was left or separated from its parents. I hope that my research will contribute to a better understanding of what led to so many children, particularly girls, being separated from the families into which they were born and then, in some cases, taken to state orphanages and sent into international adoption.

A related but somewhat separate motivation for writing about this research is a desire to tell the stories of a little-known group of rural people who struggled to form their families in an era of strict birth planning and rapid social and economic change. Our original research plan was focused on studying orphanages tasked with caring for increasing numbers of abandoned or otherwise relinquished children in the 1990s; had we proceeded with this plan we would have met few of the actual parents involved in the phenomena we wanted to understand. But, as luck would have it, as soon as we started our research the orphanages were suddenly closed to us due to the government's reaction to negative international publicity stirred by the aforementioned British film exposé of the wretched conditions that existed in Chinese state orphanages and a published report on Chinese orphanages by Human Rights Watch Asia called *Death by Default: A Policy of Fatal Neglect* that alleged the government intentionally killed children living in its orphanages.[5] As a result we had to look outside the orphanages to learn about the causes of an apparent increase in abandonment and its consequences for the children involved. Turning directly to the villages and towns where abandoned children were reportedly coming from, we quickly found many families who not only relinquished children under duress but also many more who spontaneously adopted these children without them ever reaching the hands of the government. These are the parents whose stories form the basis of this book, parents who have been largely invisible and voiceless in accounts of international adoption.

My role as an adoptive mother has positioned me as an empathetic audience for the Chinese adoptive parents and birth parents I have met as part of this study. In addition, years of interviewing predisposes a researcher to empathize with the people who share their stories by virtue of trying to understand them through their own words and experiences as they recount them. It is my hope that I have done justice to their stories as I try to provide an account of the experiences of parents and children caught in the population policy currents of this era, presenting the challenges and dilemmas people faced without whitewashing the ethical breaches and negative consequences of their choices and actions for the children involved. It is not my intention to present a "balanced" or complete picture of the operation and impact of birth planning in these areas, if such is even possible. Rather I look at those policies through a particularly critical lens, one informed by over two decades of research on their human impact, and try to illustrate my analysis with stories from rural parents who relinquished, adopted, and hid children as a direct outcome of harsh birth planning policies.

Most of this research has been a collaborative effort with Chinese colleagues who have ventured into the countryside with me for over fifteen years talking to adoptive and relinquishing parents, using their networks of kin, former and present students, and friends to lead us into networks of adoptive families as well as families who abandoned or otherwise relinquished children. My gratitude to them is enormous. My views have been profoundly shaped by them and their perspectives, which like mine changed significantly as we learned from those who shared their lives, and often their profound pain, with us. I feel a heavy responsibility to them as a whole and to some of them in particular. One of these colleagues, Wang Liyao, a senior researcher at the Anhui Academy of Social Sciences, was particularly important to the work presented in this book. Sadly, he fell ill and died before this manuscript was finished. As a co-researcher of this book, he was central to the research and, although he is not responsible for the writing of this book or specific views I have expressed, his sensibilities infuse its spirit and inform my interpretations of the material and what we learned together.

Huang Banghan, former dean of the School of Humanities and Social Sciences at Anhui Agricultural University, was crucial to the origins of my work on abandonment and adoption in the mid-1990s, providing a home base and initiating a methodology that allowed us to investigate this topic outside of official channels when our initial plans were dashed by the withdrawal of official approval for our study. With Professor Huang's help and resourcefulness, what seemed at first like a huge setback to our research turned out to be a blessing in disguise, leading us to meet hundreds of families in the villages and towns whose experiences would have otherwise remained invisible to us. In this way we were able to learn directly from parents what children were relinquished and why. We also discovered a large pool of local adopters who quickly absorbed most of the healthy children relinquished by others, usually without ever involving orphanages or even government knowledge. Finally, we were able to gain a window on families who concealed children, for brief or extended periods, and some of the consequences of doing so. None of these phenomena would have been visible to us had we studied the problems of infant abandonment through the lens of the orphanages. My tenacious and resourceful collaborators were central to turning adversity into opportunity and a much more valuable research project.

CHAPTER I

Introduction: Somebody's Children

Laura Briggs notes at the beginning of her book *Somebody's Children: The Politics of Transracial Adoption* that her goal is to "narrate a history of adoption that pays as much attention to the position of those who lose children in adoption as to those who receive them," noting that the conditions under which mothers "lost their children into adoption are rather more troubling and, indeed, violent" than most accounts lead one to believe.[1] My intention is similar. Like Briggs, I believe the historical record of adoption from China shows that the conditions that created a large pool of healthy adoptable children in the 1990s and early 2000s, both inside and outside the state orphanages, were more troubling and, indeed, more violent than most accounts of adoption from China indicate. I also, like Briggs, want to stress that these are indeed "somebody's children," children who were turned into "nobody's children" through an involuntary process that most often originated in political coercion and fear. Until recently, most accounts of international adoption from China have been written by or for international adoptive parents who, in turn, pass on the account as they know it to their adopted children.[2] The voices and perspectives of Chinese birth parents, those who lost the children adopted by others, are largely absent. Also absent in these accounts, indeed wholly invisible, is another group in China that is crucial to this history, the Chinese adoptive parents of children in the same cohort as those who are sent into international adoption, the Chinese counterparts of international adoptive parents.[3] Part of the unknown troubling history of Chinese adoption involves the losses and travails, as well as the unexpected gains, of this group, standing alongside the unmitigated losses of Chinese birth parents.

Drawing on the experiences of the parents we interviewed, this short book examines the various and changing ways used to conceal "illegal children" over three decades of China's one-child policy, a policy first implemented in the Chinese countryside at the beginning of the 1980s. Although known generically as the one-child policy throughout this period, in most rural areas, including our research area, the policy was modified by the late 1980s to allow a second birth several years after the birth of a girl, becoming a one-son-or-two-child policy, also known as a 1.5-child policy. As villagers sought to maintain some control over their reproduction and the formation of their families in the face of these policies, the main objects of the struggle between families and local representatives of state power were children, the products of reproduction that the state sought to limit. As Tyrene White conceptualized this era, it was characterized by a struggle between a powerful, determined state and a "strong society" that had some ability in the villages to resist, although at a high cost to those involved.[4] Our study provides support for this understanding of a struggle between state and society but modifies White's notion that family patriarchy, manifested in families' determination to have a son, singularly spearheaded and shaped this struggle between state and society. In contrast to White and many others, we find strong desires among many families to also have or obtain daughters, often above and beyond what was allowed by the state. Families resisted not only for the sake of a son but also for a widespread two child–two gender ideal, a pattern that we saw most clearly in patterns of adoption. Studies indicate that in some rural areas up to the mid-1990s, over 30 percent resisted the dictates of policy by having unauthorized births and hiding them from the government in one way or another.[5] These hidden births include many daughters who remain members of their birth families without government knowledge as well as many who were welcomed as daughters into local adoptive families.

Parent strategies that emerged in this struggle involved hiding pregnancies and children in various ways, many of which resulted in circulating children surreptitiously among rural Chinese families of friends and strangers, a pattern that eventually came to include the families of international adopters via state orphanages.[6] In order to avoid birth planning punishments and constraints—implemented in the 1980s and 1990s in fierce, sometimes violent campaigns that waxed and waned, and in the 2000s through strictly enforced routinized top-down administrative controls—children were frequently hidden through local adoption, infant abandonment, and various forms of concealment and disguise. When discovered by or taken to local authorities, some of these children passed into government welfare institutions and state-run orphanages. In the 1990s when female infant abandonment and other efforts to hide children were widespread, Chinese state orphanages temporarily filled, leading to government policies that expanded the local circulation of rural Chinese children globally to international adopters through the state orphanage system.[7] Simultaneously, as we shall see, the state sought to restrict the domestic circulation of children by suppressing local adoption, a long-standing customary practice in many rural areas, including the area where we conducted research. An unknown number of the healthy children that were put into the international adoption pool were taken directly from local adoptive families who hoped to raise them as their own daughters, while many other prospective adopters were prevented from adopting the children who ended up in orphanages. Eventually, more than 120,000 children would be sent by Chinese state orphanages into international adoption over two decades, an indirect product of the twin policies of restricting births and suppressing domestic adoption because of the latter's role in concealing births from birth planners. The suppression of local and customary adoption, launched in the service of shoring up birth planning regulations, has persisted through the last three decades, appearing with renewed vigor in recent years as a central policy in the control of "child trafficking," even though, as we will show, this policy has itself led to charges of child trafficking leveled at government officials.

Previous and Current Research

The circulation of rural children through various forms of relinquishment and adoption has been the focus of over fifteen years of study conducted in central China[8] with the collaboration of Chinese colleagues. The material upon which this book is based incorporates information gathered through in-depth interviews and questionnaires administered to over 350 parents who permanently relinquished children through abandonment, around one thousand Chinese families who adopted children in this era, and over eight hundred families who hid children through nonregistration, avoiding a record of the child's birth and existence. Families in these categories were located by following networks of friends, relatives, and contacts in a snowball fashion. Most of the information therefore comes from one central province and adjacent areas, although a minority of the questionnaires and interviews tapped into more distant networks in other parts of the country. Most of the questionnaires were administered by a team of Chinese researchers, their students, and their contacts and were gathered between 1996 and 2002. Since that time I have continued visiting and interviewing in the same area, sometimes returning to the same families, with the help of one or more Chinese colleagues. I have also interviewed people in a few other areas. Throughout this time I participated in most of the in-depth interviews, usually alongside one of my Chinese colleagues, interviewing several hundred adoptive families and abandoning or relinquishing families, including families who had children forcibly seized from them by local government officials. In addition I have talked to hundreds of families, casually and in interviews, who have hidden children through various means involving nonregistration or false registration.

I have reported much of the information gathered between 1996 and 2002 in previously published articles and an expanded and revised edited collection of these articles in 2004.[9] This book incorporates the follow-up research that we have done since the completion of the earlier research and focuses on previously unpublished in-depth interview material and fieldwork observations collected over the past fifteen years. Woven into my analysis of three decades of child circulation under the one-child policy are the narrative stories of Chinese parents and children who have shared their experiences with us during this time. The range of topics encompassed under the rubric of the concealment and circulation of children — abandonment/relinquishment, adoption, and nonregistration/irregular registration — provides a lens for viewing the impact on local society of the world's longest and most massive population control project, focusing on rural families and their children.

Out-of-Plan Children

Almost all of the children we learned about fell into a category defined by government policy as "out of plan," meaning children who were born in violation of the local birth planning rules at the time, rules that specify timing as well as number of permitted births.[10]

"Planned" children, those born according to the rules with official permission, or born "in plan," were generally not involved in any of these practices, indicating the great extent to which government population policy defines and shapes the fate of children born in this era. Most children born out of plan, without official permission, begin life as unregistered children, popularly known as *hei-haizi*, or "black children," children who lack household registration, or *hukou*, and thereby lack an official existence. Some remain in this category throughout childhood, particularly adopted children, as many regulations make difficult or even prohibit the registration of out-of-plan children.[11] However, most children that we learned about eventually obtained registration in the form of a hukou using various means, including the creation of false identities. The patterns of circulation and concealment that emerge are complex and changing, as both society and policies interact and change over the three-plus decades of the one-child policy. The stories presented in this book are chosen to suggest the evolving patterns of evasion and resistance in response to changing policy, forms of coercion and circumstances, illustrating the human consequences for those involved. Despite significant socioeconomic changes and modest policy modifications, the heavy costs of the policies and the impact they have had on people's lives persist and reverberate over this period and for many people will continue for the rest of their lives.

Unintended costs and negative consequences such as the world's most skewed sex ratios reported at birth, the creation of a future bachelor population, and a rapidly aging population structure, have been studied and analyzed by many researchers, mostly at a macro-level.[12] This book focuses above all on individual human costs of the population project in rural areas, not just the most dramatic individual costs that receive periodic publicity, such as the forced late-term abortion of Feng Jianmei that "went viral" on the Internet in June 2012,[13] but also costs that are less visible and poorly documented, costs borne by relatively powerless and voiceless rural parents and children. The consequences they have suffered have been largely ignored or misrepresented by the government that designed the project and have been unseen by many who have studied the policies.[14] The international China adoption community, which has benefited from these policies, indeed exists only as a result of these policies, has also been relatively uninformed about the costs to rural families and children described here. Our gains have come directly as a result of the losses suffered by Chinese families.

Beyond the "Dying Rooms" and "the Deeply Unwanted, Unvalued Baby"

As our research proceeded in the 1990s, I realized that our findings challenged the beliefs and understandings of the growing US adoption community in many ways.[15] China and Chinese culture is often cast in US popular images and writing as vastly different and alien to "our way of thinking," a kind of dichotomous "other" to European and US society and culture.[16] Nowhere has the American proclivity to cast Chinese as our "others" and see China and the United States in dichotomous terms been clearer than in the public discourse on China adoption. In this context, the British documentary *The Dying Rooms: Asia's Darkest Secret*, first aired on Britain's Channel 4 in 1995 just as my colleagues and I were beginning this research, presented a sensationalized expose of Chinese orphanages where, they claimed, children were left to die. The film not only criticized the government for failing to provide minimal care for infants in their institutions, a not unreasonable charge, but even more so it excoriated Chinese culture, as the filmmakers and much of their audience imagined it. Filmed vérité style with hidden cameras, co-director Kate Blewett is filmed in an iconic moment unwrapping a swaddled infant lying in an orphanage crib to expose her genitals to the camera to prove "it really is only girls who are rejected," having previously commented that here in the orphanages was proof that Chinese do indeed "dump [baby girls] on the streets like kittens in a bag." This film was criticized at the time by some of the first US adoptive parents of Chinese children, including myself, as sensationalistic and one-sided,[17] being replete with dark Oriental-sounding music evoking evil and filled with gratuitous images sure to appall a US and European audience, such as a puppy being skinned at a food market in Guangzhou. But the film's images resonated with a US popular imagination about China and influenced many potential adopters to choose China as a place to adopt, a place where they imagined untold numbers of abject discarded girls were waiting to be rescued from a country that did not want them and brought into a loving American family.[18]

As American adoption of Chinese children grew in the 1990s, adoption agencies and editorial writers alike marveled at how readily unwanted Chinese girls found loving homes in America, juxtaposing this to the alternative of languishing in the "dying rooms" of Chinese orphanages, unwanted and unloved in their country of birth. In April 1993, the *New York Times Magazine* featured on its cover a China adoption story with the byline "How Li Sha, Abandoned in Wuhan, Became Hannah Porter, Embraced in Greenwich Village," placed under a full-page photo of a healthy, beautifully dressed baby Hannah.[19] Over a decade later, in 2004, a Fourth of July editorial by Ellen Goodman about her granddaughter Cloe, recently adopted from China, celebrated an American culture that welcomed these Chinese girls as newcomers to the American family while echoing the common view that "in China an ancient culture that still sets a higher value on the head of a boy has collided with a government policy that pressures families to have only one child. As a result, hundreds of thousands of girls . . . faced the options of either an orphanage or America."[20] Goodman stressed that through adoption to the United States, the "entire arc of [Cloe's] short life had gone from being abandoned to being treasured," "embraced with a loyalty that is all the more tenacious for having not been preordained by biology." In Goodman's Fourth of July vignette, as in Bruce Porter's story of rescue, the progressive American example shone as bright as the proverbial beacon on the hill.[21]

The construction of the "unwanted abandoned girl child" has continued to be steady fare after more than two decades of international adoption from China. In January 2014, an adoptive US mother, a medical doctor, writing about her recent adoption stated that she knew her daughter's likely history before she went to pick her up, that she was adopting a child who, due to the "conjunction of law and culture is a deeply unwanted, unvalued baby," indeed a tragedy.[22]

In this discourse, as in others involving international adoption,[23] the "unwanted abandoned girl" readily becomes the center of parental love in an adoptive home abroad, casting families and parents in the United States and China in starkly different ways. Adoption agencies assured US adopters that unlike Americans and other Westerners who opened their hearts to these abandoned children from a distant and very different land, welcoming them into the intimate spaces of their families "as their own," Chinese were unwilling to adopt the discarded female children of strangers due to the strong traditional influence of patriarchal disdain for girls and an equally strong devotion to family bloodlines. In this discourse, Chinese culture, almost singularly characterized by Confucian son preference and patrilineal bloodlines, is foregrounded in explanations for why Chinese parents "choose" not to parent girls. Elements of this discourse can also be found echoed among Chinese involved in or writing about international adoption, reinforcing its validity in the minds of international adopters.[24]

In contrast to this discourse and the pervasive narrative of the "unwanted Chinese girl," the research discussed here shows that many Chinese wanted to adopt girls and that persistent son preference did not preclude the desire for daughters, even among those who felt pressured to relinquish girls under the harsh coercion of birth planning campaigns. No doubt Goodman's granddaughter Cloe, like my own daughter and many others, was deeply treasured by her American family, but we learned that the "arc from being abandoned to being treasured" might also be traversed within the same village, county, or region in China. This fact is an important counterweight to the deeply held notion that international adoptive parents were their children's "only hope" and to adopted children's belief that they were "unwanted in China." Furthermore, we learned that the main obstacle to even more relinquished children like Cloe finding permanent new families as wanted daughters in their own communities was a persistent government effort to prevent relinquished "out-of-plan" children from being adopted locally through customary adoption practices rather than being channeled into a state orphanage, institutions that are notoriously ill suited to meeting the needs of young children. Had it not been for these government efforts to prevent local adoption, healthy girls would have never filled the state orphanages in this area of China.

One of the purposes of this book is to provide the adopted children who grow up in America with a more complex, evidence-based picture of the place from which they were taken and the government policies that led to this outcome. Learning more about people in China who adopted as well as those who relinquished out-of-plan girls in the same cohort as those adopted to North America and Europe will hopefully create a fuller and more complex picture than the standard discourse about unwanted abandoned girls presents. The very existence of tens of thousands of adoptive parents of abandoned girls in China flies in the face of the images of Chinese culture that are typically found in the United States where the majority of internationally adopted Chinese girls are being raised. The research presented in this book shows that many of the abandoned children who remained in China did not languish in orphanages, as postulated by Ellen Goodman, US adoption agencies, and many US adoptive parents. Indeed, hundreds of thousands of abandoned girls were directly, if secretly, adopted locally without ever entering an orphanage, while thousands of those who did enter state orphanages were also adopted domestically, despite the restrictions placed on those allowed to adopt.[25] These girls have grown up as wanted and valued daughters in Chinese adoptive families just as the internationally adopted girls have grown up as valued daughters in adoptive families in the United States, Canada, and Europe.[26] We learned the vast majority of Chinese adoptions take place outside of orphanages and most go unregistered due to a highly restrictive adoption law that makes it difficult to register many adoptions, especially adoptions that take place outside of orphanages. Yet even among legally registered adoptions, which includes all adoptions from state orphanages, international adoption never exceeded 30 percent even at its peak in 2005 when around fourteen thousand children, mostly healthy young girls, were adopted internationally from Chinese orphanages, after which the numbers dropped steadily and the composition of adoptees became older, less healthy, and more gender balanced.[27]

The fairly widespread existence of domestic adoption throughout this era is a fact not well known even in China, especially in urban China, where adoptions are often hidden for a variety of reasons, including the need to hide adoptions from birth planning officials. Unlike international adopters who are racially different than their adopted child, Chinese adopters often have a choice to pass as biological parents, something most international adopters in North America and Europe cannot do. Indeed, international adopters are under some pressure to explain their family to others due to the obvious racial difference. In the United States white adoptive parents often make a virtue of this necessity by extolling the virtues of "openness" in adoption. Here too Chinese who are "secretive" may be found lacking relative to international adopters.[28] Nonetheless, adoption is no less common or any more stigmatized in Chinese society than in the United States and, according to family historians, was actually more common than in North America and Europe in the past.[29]

One of the main arguments that grows out of this research is that adoption regulations and laws that sought to suppress customary domestic Chinese adoption for the purpose of shoring up the enforcement of birth planning policies contributed significantly to the conditions that gave rise to international adoption by channeling a large pool of adoptable healthy infants into the hands of the government rather than allowing more of them to find homes with local families who wanted to adopt them. The national adoption law passed in 1991, the first of its kind, codified the regulations used by birth planning officials to prevent and punish people for using adoption to circulate and hide out-of-plan births. This law restricted adoption in two ways: it made it illegal for parents to relinquish a child except under extraordinary and rare circumstances, making outright "abandonment" the only way most parents could relinquish a child; and it restricted the adoption of any relinquished child, including an "abandoned child," to a narrow pool of older adopters over thirty-five years old and still childless. Significantly, true "orphans" whose parents were deceased were exempt from these restrictions, as were disabled children. In this way, the law overtly discriminated against children who, through no fault of their own, were relinquished or abandoned, the latter involving children who were most likely born out of plan and whose births were being hidden from local authorities. Thus while an "orphan" could be adopted by any family member, friend, or other unrelated person regardless of age and number of children, "abandoned children" who were adopted by parents under thirty-five or by those who already had children could be taken from their family by the government at any time, and placed in an institution to wait until a different legally qualified person might adopt them from government hands, entering yet another family. That the purpose of such a law was to shore up birth planning regulations and strengthen government control over relinquished children is obvious; that it utterly disregarded the interests of the children concerned should be equally obvious, although this has seemed invisible to those involved in the business of institutionalizing these children. We will see in the stories that follow in this book how in practice this law did indeed put out-of-plan children at risk of losing a second family after already having lost a birth family.

Thus we find that two related sets of policies and laws—the birth planning laws generically known as the one-child policy[30] and the 1991 national adoption law—together led to increased abandonment and availability of healthy out-of-plan children in the hands of the government in the 1990s and early 2000s. In this context, the turn to international adoption in the 1990s provided homes for some healthy children caught in the orphanage system and, perhaps more importantly, provided financial support through high international adoption fees to overcrowded resource-starved welfare institutions, partially compensating Civil Affairs and its welfare system for the disastrous consequences of central birth planning and adoption policies.

Wanting a Daughter, Needing a Son:
Complicating Notions of "Son Preference"

As our research makes clear, not only has adoption in rural China been fairly common in this era, arousing determined and only partially successful government efforts to suppress this local practice, but also the adoption of daughters, in particular, has been popular and widespread in many areas.[31] Indeed, our research suggests that were it not for actively pursued policies of suppression, nearly all relinquished healthy daughters in the 1990s could have found families who wanted them in China, leaving few healthy children available for international adoption. Yet, in US and Chinese media reports, the local adoption of girls in China, when recognized at all, is usually characterized as an effort to get a child bride or "little daughter-in-law" to marry a son or perhaps obtain a family servant. Recent reports carried by wire services like Reuters claim, citing no specific evidence, that baby girls are trafficked into adoption for "lucrative dowries,"[32] apparently because the reporters or those they talk to cannot imagine why else anyone would want a daughter because allegedly girls are not valued in Chinese society and only boys are wanted for adoption. In our research, we found scant evidence of such former practices as adopting child brides or "little daughters-in-law" in this era, at least not in our research area.[33] Usually, Chinese parents' reasons for adopting children, especially daughters, were similar to international adopters. While the adoption of sons, which was relatively rare in our sample due to the small number of boys available for adoption, was often explained in terms of instrumental economic and social security needs, adopted daughters more often were said to "increase the happiness" in a family by bringing noninstrumental qualities such as closeness, love, and companionship to parents.

Not only were daughters welcomed by childless couples, girls were often specifically sought out by daughterless families that already had sons in order to "complete" the family. "A son and a daughter make a family complete" was a common saying in this area and was a family ideal that many sought either through adoption or birth, the latter perhaps occasionally aided secretly by illegal prenatal sex selection.[34] One particularly proud father who had just paid off a hefty fine for his three-year-old daughter born several years after his son, surrounded by a group of neighbors, told us that this two child–two gender ideal was an "old Chinese tradition." This was a sentiment spontaneously echoed by many rural people we talked to over the years. In contrast, we rarely heard the old expression "More sons, more happiness," a saying that is said to characterize traditional Chinese cultural attitudes, expressing strong and seemingly exclusive "son preference."[35] In our extensive research among adopters and other villagers we did not find the son-obsessed patriarchs portrayed by Mo Yan and Ma Jian in their novels about birth planning, and by many other writers and reporters, although no doubt they exist.[36]

Indeed, we found overtly expressed "son preference" to be relatively weak among the adopters we met; "daughter preference" was more common in this particular group of adopters, notably among those who already had a son, a group that comprised half of all adopters in our sample.[37] Childless adopters most often claimed that either gender was fine, with a few preferring girls because of the presumed closeness of daughters to parents. Only a small minority said explicitly that they would have preferred to adopt a boy but settled on adopting a girl because no boys were available. Anecdotally, we also found a predictable desire for daughters among those who had illegal overquota pregnancies after having a son, such as the father mentioned above, whether or not they achieved their hoped-for outcome. While the onset of birth planning, along with the nearly simultaneous collapse of the (meager) rural social safety net and reemergence of household land use rights, seems in some ways to have revived patriarchal male gender preferences, bringing a halt to the progress of previous decades toward greater gender equality,[38] a closer look shows that new values and attitudes toward gender continued to evolve or even accelerated in this period, even in the midst of increasingly skewed reported sex ratios at birth.[39] Indeed, the rural area in central China where we interviewed and found these evolving attitudes toward daughters recorded some of the most skewed reported sex ratios in China.[40] Nonetheless, these positive attitudes toward daughters surfaced in the adoption patterns we found and in the strong desire of those with a son to also have a daughter. Notably, and importantly, the reported sex ratio skew at birth occurred here, as elsewhere in rural areas, only among second or higher births to those who already had daughters but no sons. This is a pattern fully compatible with a two-gender family ideal, not merely a pattern reflecting simple "son preference."

While our research was among the first to document these changing attitudes toward daughters in adoption practices,[41] these findings resonate with many other studies that have found increasingly positive attitudes toward daughters in rural China in the 1980s and 1990s as the desire for more than one son waned and disappeared.[42] This clear trend parallels the increasing value and status of "singleton," or only-child, urban daughters in the era of the one-child policy, a phenomenon that has been well documented by Vanessa Fong.[43]

A strong desire for sons, often expressed as a "need," was, of course, found among the segment of the population that abandoned or otherwise relinquished girls for the sake of having a son. As suggested above, the felt need for a son was perhaps heightened by the disappearance of any collective welfare in the 1980s around the same time that birth planning restrictions were spreading in the countryside. During the first three decades of the one-child policy and post-Mao economic boom, the government did little to address the lack of a rural safety net and affordable health care system, even as it pushed relentlessly to lower rural birth rates. Thus, given the persistence of patrilocal marriage patterns, sons (and hopefully their wives) were the only source of social security at the same time birth restrictions significantly reduced the chances of producing one, unless people struggled against the limits and made hard choices for their families. As a village leader in Henan put it, "Those in Beijing who made these policies all have their pensions. Have any offered to give them up? They ask us to give up our [pursuit of] sons, for the sake of the nation. And we must make the villagers do the same. They hate us."[44]

Yet even under these highly unfavorable policy conditions, the evident "son preference" manifest in rising female infant abandonment was conditional; daughters were relinquished only in particular limited circumstances. In our sample of around 350 parents who abandoned daughters, all but a handful were sonless couples that already had one or more daughters.[45] More importantly, even relinquishing a second-, third-, or fourth-born daughter usually occurred only under conditions of strong external pressure to limit births under threats of severe punishments, as occurred during birth planning campaigns, and when the pregnancy itself was "out of plan" and proceeding without a permission certificate. Periods between campaigns appear to have seen sharp drops in abandonment. Learning more about the conditions under which birth parents abandoned daughters, most notably the coercive constraints they faced and had to weigh against other difficult circumstances, allowed us to better understand their decisions and to contextualize "son preference" as an explanation for the rise of female abandonment. Although rarely do the parents that abandoned or surreptitiously relinquished girls emerge as pure victims, we did not find any "voluntary relinquishments." Most were anguished. Although in some cases officials simply took out-of-plan children from birth parents against their will, as well as from many adoptive parents, most cases of relinquishment by birth parents involved what might be oxymoronically referred to as a "coerced choice." Were it not for birth planning threats and constraints, these parents would not have relinquished, let alone abandoned, their daughters no matter how many they had. Culturally, the pursuit of a son through multiple births did not require jettisoning daughters.

Indeed, most parents, caught in the squeeze between the state's harsh demands and their own needs and desires, found ways to hold on to both the girls and boys they gave birth to, even those who were out of plan, although often with great difficulty and sometimes great cost. Certainly, one of the main causes of rural impoverishment during these decades was the mandatory payment for out-of-plan children that many parents had to hand over to the government for the right to register and raise their children, often in amounts that far exceeded their annual income. Not surprisingly, many parents hid children. In a study of unregistered "black children" conducted between 2000 and 2003, we learned about several hundred hidden children who were neither abandoned nor permanently adopted out of their families, in addition to hundreds of hidden children living in adoptive families.[46] Those who did abandon a child did so in the face of imminent threats, including government-imposed impoverishment and forced sterilization, a feared and painful procedure, which additionally brought to an end all hopes for a son.

The plight of these parents was palpable. This generation of parents, the first to find the heavy boot of birth planning come down hard on their necks, at a time that rural fertility desires, though rapidly declining, had just recently fallen below three, was forced to grapple with new ethical challenges posed by the sudden onset of fierce birth planning campaigns and then live with the consequences of the compromises they made.[47] Because there was usually a "choice" made, some degree of personal agency exercised in the act of resisting the restrictions and avoiding the material and corporeal punishments imposed on them, one of the consequences was living with guilt and remorse in addition to loss. In over fifteen years of research and interviews, some repeated years later, we have learned that abandonment of a child often casts a long shadow over the lives of those who have made this coerced choice, leaving a permanent hole in a family where a child should be. Living with regret was part of the price imposed by this kind of coerced choice.

The Centrality of Policy and Government-Sanctioned Coercion

The portrait of the central Chinese government and its policies that emerges from this research is, for the most part, unrelentingly negative, presenting a picture of determined efforts to impose top-down control over people's reproductive behavior despite the enormous human costs, including, indeed especially, costs to children.[48] For rural people in the 1980s and 1990s the demands of the center were extreme and their actions harsh. Officials at the bottom sometimes created room for maneuver by lessening punishments, looking the other way, or accepting bribes in lieu of enforcement, thereby making the system more flexible and humane at times. Some of the areas where we conducted interviews, known for pervasive local corruption, were notoriously lax in implementing the birth planning policies of higher levels. In these areas, corruption worked in favor of parents who had out-of-plan children. But systemic pressures from above frequently punished and overwhelmed local efforts to soften the harsh policies set in Beijing that were forwarded through the provinces with only minor revisions. A typical example comes from Longhui, Hunan, where in the late 1990s, some local officials tried to protect villagers from an outside birth planning team by warning pregnant women to hide and hiring men to pretend they were recovering from vasectomies. Exposed by a reporter, the low-level officials were punished.[49] Village leaders were limited in their ability to deflect top-down demands and all too often succumbed to the pressures to swing far in the opposite direction of extreme implementation to try to correct their lax records in birth planning work. Thus, a few years later Longhui becomes the epicenter of a media scandal involving harsh official behavior "kidnapping children for ransom," a scandal we will examine in depth.

In the 2000s, administrative policies such as the "one vote veto rule" (*yipiao foujue zhidu*), a policy first introduced in the early 1990s, that holds local officials responsible for out-of-plan births, became more firmly institutionalized and regularized in many local areas, reducing both the periods of laxness and the periodic campaign strikes of the 1990s. Yet in the stories we heard on the ground, the policies in the 2000s remained very strict even if less erratic up through the 2010 census and beyond. These policies continued to create strong pressures that put out-of-plan children at risk in various ways and sometimes separated children from families, as shown by the Longhui case and several others we will examine later in depth, even as actual infant abandonment declined and almost disappeared in most areas.

This study's focus on those who have suffered the loss of children or who struggled to keep them in the face of fearful punishments and threats emanating from the policies and administrative apparatus of a powerful government inevitably focuses us on the coercive, perverse, and cruel impact of population policies on rural families and rural children who were born out of plan, policies that make the very existence of these unauthorized children illegal. That these policies carried a vision of a better, modern future, that in urban areas, which now constitute half of the population, they have evolved far (although not fully) from their coercive origins, does not resonate in the accounts given here. This research uncovers a segment of the population that has been punished, "left behind," and in some cases literally pushed out of the country, by the processes and policies that were intended to cultivate modern, educated global citizens in twenty-first-century China.[50] Despite resilience among many who have suffered, the losses have been great even if unseen and unacknowledged.

The Role of Legal Coercion in International Adoption

Somewhat surprisingly, the culpability of state-sanctioned coercion in separating children from their parents is rarely recognized in discussions of international adoption, although as we will see government coercion sits at the center of China's international adoption program, a program that has provided the world's largest pool of children for international adoption since the mid-1990s. While the one-child policy is usually seen as a background factor, the question of why there are children available to adopt in China turns quickly to the question of "why girls?"—a question that firmly centers the discussion on Chinese culture as the primary, most culpable factor responsible for the pool of children available for international adoption. Similarly, studies of international adoptive parent narratives find that notions of Chinese culture are often prominently centered in trying to construct stories of their children's origins, origins that are otherwise shrouded in mystery due to the circumstances of abandonment and the near total absence of Chinese birth parent voices.[51] Perhaps the absent role of policy and state power in many of these narratives is partly because this subject or its implicit harshness is considered inappropriate for children. It may also be because the earlier litany that comprised what Susan Greenhalgh has dubbed the "coercion narrative" in US media accounts of the one-child policy gave way in the late 1990s to a new, and ultimately misleading, narrative about the moderation of China's population policy, emphasizing the emergence of a new focus on reproductive health, better quality services, and education along with more lawful implementation in place of the earlier waves of coercive campaigns.[52] From the late 1990s, media reports declared the end or imminent demise of the one-child policy almost every year. This change in coverage occurred around the time that international adoption was taking off. Under these conditions, a kind of "voluntary relinquishment" might be imagined, with Chinese cultural attitudes being seen as the primary reasons that tradition-bound and still relatively poor rural birth parents "chose" to give up female children through abandonment or other forms of relinquishment.[53] This kind of cultural explanation also dovetailed with relatively common images of Chinese society discussed earlier and finds parallels in other cases of transnational adoption.[54]

The absence of birth parent voices has also given more room for the dominant "cultural narrative" to hold sway in understandings of adoption from China. The birth parent voices presented here clearly and painfully center the role of policy and coercion in their narratives, hopefully correcting the prevailing narratives constructed by international adoptive parents, adoption agencies, and the Chinese government.

Even critics of international adoption and those concerned with evaluating and monitoring the terms of the Hague Convention on intercountry adoption and the rights of the child, a convention that is supposed to govern adoption from China, have barely blinked at the broadly coercive government policies that lay behind the creation of the supply of Chinese children for international adoption, focusing instead on regulating illegal behavior, corruption, and trafficking for profit in adoption.[55] While in China the latter behavior may be the perverse outcome of the policies that will be discussed here, legally sanctioned policies and laws lie at the center of most of these problems and give rise to behavior that many observers label "corrupt," partly because they do not understand the laws and how they operate. Indeed, while the Hague Convention bans criminal abduction and the use of "compensation or payment" in adoption, and prioritizes domestic placement over international placement,[56] something the Chinese program has never done due to laws that suppress most domestic adoption, the convention fails to mention as ethically problematic legal policies that severely punish and impoverish people for producing children, policies that induce parents to relinquish children under duress, children they would otherwise keep. While trafficking for profit is understandably a serious concern of Hague Convention lawyers and international adoption critics, legally sanctioned punishments, including huge financial levies against parents that in effect put a price on the head of every child born "outside the plan," are left virtually invisible by this convention and the discussions about the ethics of international adoption that it has generated.[57] This blindness, in turn, makes invisible the way these policies fuel the kind of child trafficking that the Hague Convention hopes to prevent, policies that generate a supply of children for this trade as well as the pool of healthy children that has been available for international adoption. Also downplayed in favor of a focus on the cash nexus of international adoption is the role of sanctioned government coercion and laws in reinforcing the enormous inequalities between Chinese birth parents who lose children and international adopters who gain them, including the plenary adoption laws embodied in the Hague Convention itself that accept "abandonment" as a form of "voluntary relinquishment" in lieu of an informed consent that severs all birth parent rights.

Government policy, however harsh, and the ethical issues it creates for those who are involved in China's international adoption program are thereby oddly downplayed if not absent in the narratives of international adoption by all of the major voices shaping the public discourse.

Population Control in the Politics of Climate Change

The tendency to downplay criticism of the role of government coercion in the creation of a pool of adoptable children made available to international adopters may also be related to widespread sympathy for the project of limiting China's population growth for the sake of addressing the world's ecological crises. The Chinese government claims the one-child policy has saved China and the world from 400 million additional people to feed, educate, transport, and power in an ecologically fragile world, a claim that resonates with international concerns for the planet's future. This claim is greatly exaggerated, if not entirely bogus.[58] Yet even if China's population is somewhat lower today or will level off in the future at a slightly lower level due to this policy, this reduction must be judged against the high costs it has exacted from the generations that have borne the brunt of the policy and those who will live with its long-term negative consequences. Before accepting "population control" as part of the mix of policies intended to combat climate change and ecological destruction,[59] we will do well to look long and hard at those consequences as a cautionary tale of what happens at the extremes.

What follows in this book is an effort to give voice to those most affected and to document some of the lesser known and largely invisible negative consequences of these policies for the daily lives and family relationships of a segment of the rural population. The individual human costs shown here should be added to the better known demographic costs of China's population policies—skewed sex ratios, rapid population aging, the creation of a bachelor population—as well as the diffuse political costs of mounting and maintaining coercive policies that periodically surface in publicized cases of brutal coercion against individuals and continue to provoke pockets of overt and violent resistance in some rural areas in the face of crackdowns.[60] Beneath all of this, the abrogation of parental rights and, even worse, the citizenship rights of out-of-plan children, the main collateral damage of the government's policy, has left deep if often invisible scars across Chinese society. As we will see, the Chinese state and its local agents not only put enforcement of its birth planning policies above the welfare of children but also implemented administrative policies that often compelled local officials to willfully act against the interests of specific children in pursuit of meeting population quotas or else suffer severe penalties themselves. Given these patterns, negative effects of population policies such as infant abandonment, overcrowded orphanages that provided inadequate care for young children's health and development, and the creation of a large group of children who have been deprived of citizenship, often as a means of punishing parents, cannot reasonably be seen as merely "unintended consequences" of population policies but rather their logical and sometimes intentional effects.

The next two chapters, chapters 2 and 3, relate specific examples of families who relinquished, adopted, and variously hid out-of-plan children in an effort to build their families in the face of formidable obstacles and fearsome punishments created by birth planning policy enforced by the disciplinary power of a state that is able to reach to the bottom of society. Chapters 4 and 5 consider how recent concerns of "child trafficking" are related to the birth planning and adoption policies discussed in earlier chapters and their consequences under conditions of low but uneven fertility, focusing on how these policies have allowed, even encouraged, local officials to take children from families that wanted to raise them. Thus what has sometimes appeared as corrupt and illegal behavior by local officials caught participating in kidnapping, trafficking, and selling children into international or domestic adoption may be seen more accurately and critically as behavior flowing directly from central government sanctioned laws and regulations governing fertility and adoption.

The stories presented in these chapters illustrate the problems and liabilities that have been created by the enforcement of these laws and regulations for families and children in a variety of settings and time periods over the past thirty years. Some of the cases recounted in these chapters are families that we kept in touch with and visited many times over the years. I have chosen the examples to illustrate the changing patterns of circulating and concealing children that result from strategies intended to resist or avoid birth planning demands as parents sought to build their families in ways they felt necessary for their survival, social security, and desires for children while avoiding impoverishment and other material and corporeal punishments threatened by the government, including the seizure of their "illegal" children.

CHAPTER 2

Relinquishing Daughters—from Customary
Adoption to Abandonment

The stories of child relinquishment[1] in the 1980s and 1990s that we gathered illustrate families' ways of resisting and negotiating shifting local birth planning policies as the surveillance and regulation of births and adoptions progressively deepened over the first two decades of the one-child policy. By the 1990s, relinquishment of a child through adoption or any other means was made illegal in the national adoption law except in rare cases, forcing people to turn to more anonymous and riskier forms of giving up a child in order to hide a birth. The patterns that emerge from these stories illustrate the long reach and profound effect of these birth planning and adoption policies on basic human relationships in China's families and villages, as well as the resilience of villagers in pursuing their own changing desires and perceived needs in the face of these new policies. The stories also reveal that this pursuit has a heavy human cost, borne by both parents and, above all, children, who are the powerless objects of the lopsided negotiations and evasions that parents must engage in to avoid the often fearsome punishments meted out by local officials trying to implement the central government's highest priority policies.

The five stories that follow show the patterns that emerge in the

wake of escalating efforts to implement policies that make open relinquishment impossible and try to restrict local adoption.

Hiding a Daughter through an Arranged Adoption

Birth mother Huang Mei[2] (b. 1964)
Husband/birth father Ding Yuan (b. 1964)
First child, daughter born 1986
Second child, daughter born June 1988, adopted-out (Ding
    Haiyan)
Third child, son born 1991

In the 1980s, one of the first strategies to evade restrictions on childbearing was to use customary adoption practices for a new purpose.
In earlier decades in this area, adoptions were arranged among
friends, relatives, and strangers, involving both girls and boys, for
a variety of reasons. Poverty was a primary reason to adopt-out an
additional child, as was helping a childless relative or close friend to
obtain a child. After the implementation of the one-child policy in
the early 1980s, the need to hide children from authorities led to a
rapid increase in the number of adoptions in this area, despite rising incomes and declining fertility, conditions that might otherwise
lead to lower rates of adoption. The story of the Huang-Ding family
illustrates a couple that felt compelled in these new circumstances to
adopt-out a second daughter that they would otherwise have raised
themselves.

Usually, those who adopted-out a child in this era had no son
and were adopting out a second or third girl in order to try again to
produce a son. Regulations against customary adoption were only
just emerging and local officials often ignored what went on out
of sight, outside of the village, especially if there was no vigorous
birth planning campaign underway. When Huang Mei,[3] a twenty-

five-year-old woman living in a small village in south central China, gave birth to her second daughter in 1988, two years after the birth of her first daughter, she never considered sending the child away, much less abandoning her, even though she hoped to try again to give birth to a son. Although their income was only average for their village, she and her husband felt they could afford to raise two daughters and still try again to have a son; she thought two daughters and a son would make a fine family. Because birth planning pressures were relatively lax in their village in the mid- to late 1980s and outside officials seemed unaware of her second pregnancy, they assumed they could keep their family together and proceed quickly with another pregnancy.

But during the first months of their second daughter's life, rumors of a new birth planning campaign began to circulate. Frightening stories of mandatory sterilization for those who had given birth to two children spread. There were rumors of people rounded up for mass procedures that were painful and dangerous; it was said that some women died. At first Huang Mei's husband, Ding Yuan, could not bear the idea of giving away their baby daughter, even in the face of these frightening rumors. Huang Mei recalled that as they discussed this, he cried. But Huang Mei feared that if they kept their second daughter, they would invariably be discovered in the approaching campaign and she might be sterilized, making it impossible to ever have a son and possibly maiming her. She was frightened by the prospect and eventually persuaded him to consider an adoption. So Huang Mei and her husband decided reluctantly to look into arranging an adoption for their baby daughter, then six months old, in order to hide her and avoid being forced to undergo sterilization. They knew that Ding Yuan's brother and sister-in-law, who had two boys, had wanted a girl. They only lived about two kilometers away on the north side of the small town where Huang Mei and Ding Yuan lived. When Huang and her husband talked to them about adopting their daughter, the daughterless couple immediately welcomed the idea; they were prohibited from another birth, so this was their best chance to have a daughter. Because they only lived a couple of kilometers away and they were close relatives, Huang Mei and her husband decided to go through with the adoption although her husband remained reluctant to let someone else, even his own brother and sister-in-law, raise his daughter. Under other circumstances they would not have done it.

So as the new birth planning campaign descended, they secretly sent their daughter to Ding Yuan's brother and his wife. A local official in his brother's village soon found out about this arrangement, but because the adoptive family knew the official well and had good relations with him he asked only for a relatively low fine of around 500 yuan (equivalent to about half their annual household income) and did not press the adoptive couple to undergo sterilization even though they now had three children. Through his good relations with officials in his area, the adoptive father was also able to get a hukou for the girl in his household soon after she moved there, even though neither family ever registered the birth of the child or the adoption. The child was named Ding Haiyan, thus carrying the surname of both her adoptive father and her birth father.

Under this arrangement, Huang Mei was given permission to have another child in two years and luckily gave birth to the son she had hoped for. Over the next few years, Huang Mei and her husband's economic situation continued to improve, and they moved into the county town. Like many other parents of the era, with an improving economic situation, they invested more in their children's education, including their first daughter's. The older daughter graduated from middle school and went on to a medical college. When their son was around fourteen and entered middle school, Huang Mei's sister-in-law suggested that Ding Haiyan live in the county town with her birth parents so she too could attend a better school, offering to contribute to the expense of her schooling. At first Huang Mei was uncertain, worried that her birth daughter would be unhappy and cold toward them. Haiyan was very close to her adoptive parents and seemed resentful toward her birth parents. Although she had recently been told who her birth mother was, she still referred to Huang Mei as her *gumu* (father's brother's wife) and continued to see her adoptive mother, her actual *gumu*, as her mother, calling her *mama*. Huang Mei felt that normal parent-child feelings and relationships could not be restored and was hesitant to disrupt Haiyan's adoptive family and try to reintegrate her into her birth family's home. But Huang Mei's husband was eager to have his birth daughter move back into their home and finally persuaded her. So Haiyan came back to live with her birth parents to go to school and was given her own room in their home. Nonetheless, she chose to spend weekends and her school vacations with her adoptive parents, where she continued to be welcome as their daughter.

When Haiyan first went to stay in her birth family's home, she was not comfortable there even though these people were familiar to her as her relatives. While she soon developed a good relationship with her older birth sister, her relationship with her younger birth brother, the younger sibling for whom she had been sent away, was strained. They frequently quarreled about small things, and Haiyan felt she was not treated fairly by her grandmother who, in Haiyan's view, always favored the spoiled boy. Perhaps the older woman was also the one responsible for sending her away. The brother felt that his newly returned cousin-turned-sister was spoiled, expecting to eat the best dishes before others and to have many things done for her. Haiyan felt that her younger brother was used to being the center of attention, especially their grandmother's, as the precious grandson. In her adoptive family, she was the youngest child and got special attention from both her parents and her two older brothers, who were in the habit of doing things for her. The living rearrangement left sibling relations frayed for several years as they gradually got used to each other and finally grudgingly became friends.

But Haiyan continued to be closer to her adoptive mother and to call her *mama* and her birth mother *gumu*. She also continued to call her birth father *jiujiu* (uncle) and her adoptive father *baba* (father). Nonetheless, Haiyan, who moved away to attend teacher's college after middle school, told Huang Mei, "When I grow up, I will treat all of you the same, and support you equally." She would be a filial daughter to two families.[4]

As a result of the impact of escalating birth planning efforts, this second daughter was thrust into a new kind of role as a hidden infant who had to be moved from one family to another in order to make room for a younger brother, a boy whom for many years she knew as her cousin. It was not surprising that the relationship between them was strained by jealousy and, on her part, some hard feelings. But in this early period of intermittent and periodically relaxed birth planning, coupled with growing prosperity, the secretly adopted-out daughter actually benefited in some surprising ways, becoming a favorite youngest child in an adoptive family that already had sons and wanted a daughter. Not until she was fourteen did she understand that her "aunt" and "uncle" had sent her away precisely because she was a girl and they wanted a son. As a young person raised in what became a kind of "open adoption" among relatives, she assumed a double obligation to two sets of parents, perhaps a heavier burden than she would ideally want. Yet she also benefited from new norms in the countryside emphasizing investment in children's education by those who could afford the investment, even in their daughters, even in an adopted-out and adopted-in daughter. In this, she was supported by the resources of two families. Haiyan's transfer as an infant to another family and her ability as a young adult to straddle both was further facilitated by the fact that her birth father and her adoptive father were brothers, sharing their surname and sharing a grandmother with both her adoptive siblings and her birth siblings, although it appears this was a mixed blessing as she chafed at grandma's favored treatment of her younger brother, a role that she had assumed in her adoptive family. At the same time, her close relationship with her *mama* and *baba* did not prevent them from suggesting she move back to her birth parents' home for the sake of her education. Whether this was perceived as a mixed message by Haiyan is hard to say.

In many ways, Haiyan's adoption was a variant of a customary adoption under new conditions of government pressure. Haiyan's uncle and aunt with two sons wanted to adopt a child of the "missing gender," and Haiyan's birth parents needed to hide her birth to preserve the chance to have a son. Although the situation created new emotional and interpersonal challenges and forced parents to make decisions they did not want to make concerning their children, it was still possible to secure a family for a hidden daughter among relatives and maintain an ongoing relationship with the adopted-out daughter, keeping her within the same kin group.

When adoptions involved relatives during this period, they often became "open adoptions" to those directly involved and were somewhat fluid, although adoptive relationships tended to hold greater salience than biological ones, as in this case. As we heard many times in this research, "The parent who raises the child has greater weight than the one who gives birth." Popular views of adoption in this area held that parenting and not biology made a family. As an adoptive father explained to us one afternoon many years later (2011), neither biology nor legal obligation would lead an adult child to stay in touch and care for aging parents in this day and age; only the affection and close relationships built in raising a child could provide such motivation. In either case, it was better to be prepared to care for yourself in old age; children were human beings and not social insurance. Other parents in the conversation readily agreed, providing numerous examples of biologically related and legally obligated children who left the village and ignored their elderly parents.

As birth planning ramped up in this area, a larger and more destructive rupture in family relationships and parent-child ties occurred. By the early 1990s, when the highly restrictive national adoption law codified earlier local regulations, cracking down on arranged adoptions became a central part of birth planning surveillance in villages, making it difficult to make the kind of arrangements that Huang Mei and her husband made for Haiyan. Even before the law was passed, local regulations tightened. Thus new more anonymous forms of relinquishment emerged, at an increasing cost to all involved. Various methods of abandonment in particular increased in this area as customary adoption practices became more difficult to arrange.

Abandoning at a Family Gate: Finding a Daughterless Family (1988)

Birth mother Gao Wanru (b. 1959)
Birth father/husband, army officer, died 2002
First child, son born 1985
Second child, daughter born 1988, abandoned at another family's doorstep

Although anonymous abandonment of out-of-plan infants increased, many birth parents secretly investigated and targeted the doorstep of those they guessed would be likely adopters, based on their knowledge of local customs and culture. Gao Wanru was among those we talked to who devised an ultimately successful plan to find an adoptive family for the baby she could not keep. When we met Wanru in 2009, an outgoing, physically fit woman who looked younger than her age, she remembered vividly what happened twenty years earlier when, at age thirty, she secretly gave birth to a forbidden out-of-plan child. A farmer and wife of a military officer, Wanru found herself pregnant with a second child in 1988 and immediately came under pressure from her family to abort the pregnancy. She and her husband had a three-year-old son and were not allowed another birth. Her husband was under particularly strict orders to obey the one-child rule imposed on all military officers' families, a group whose careers and entitlements were dependent on the state. Locally, they were expected to serve as models for an unpopular birth planning policy. Although ordinary peasants were not always closely monitored at this time, military families were. Wanru and her husband had much to lose if they were discovered with an overquota birth—her husband's high-level job, a large fine, and probably mandated sterilization for Wanru. Yet Wanru longed to have another child, hoping for a daughter, but regardless of gender wanted to keep the child she was carrying and give her son a sibling. She therefore stubbornly resisted the pressure to abort the pregnancy while she tried to think of some way to keep this baby. Alas, it proved impossible for her to come up with a "safe place" to hide the child, and in the end she could not devise a plan that would allow her to keep and raise another child without getting caught and ruining her husband's career and their family. By this time her pregnancy was in the second trimester. Years later she recalled deciding at this point, "Even if I could not give this child a home, I could nonetheless give it a life." She was afraid of an abortion this late, but above all she wanted to bring this child into the world. So against family advice, she hid herself until she secretly gave birth in her mother's home in another village.

In the meantime she and her mother searched for families that might want to adopt a child. On her mother's side, she had a close relative with a daughter who wanted a son. But what if the baby was a girl, as she had initially hoped? A family that already had a daughter was unlikely to want to adopt another. But in this area of rural China in the late 1980s and 1990s, Wanru knew that those with one or two boys might be happy to adopt a girl even if they eventually incurred a penalty. She discussed the widespread ideal of having a child of each gender, reflected in the oft-repeated expression *ernu shuang quan* (儿女双全), "a boy and a girl make a family complete." As mentioned earlier, this was an expression that we heard many times while interviewing people in the countryside in the 1990s and early 2000s. The better known traditional expression *duo zi duo fu* (多子多福), "the more sons, the more fortune," was rarely heard in our interviews or conversations except to point out that this had been popular in the past but people no longer felt that way. Too many sons were a burden, we were often told. Although the expression *yang er fang lao* (养儿防老), "raise a son for support in old age," was still heard frequently, it seemed that only one son was wanted for this purpose as fertility norms fell and the desire for a daughter increased. Some even said that daughters, especially only daughters and adopted daughters, could now also *fang lao* for those who had no sons, though this was still not easy or ideal because a girl would also be called upon to help support her husband's parents when she married.[5]

So when Wanru heard about a distant relative who had two sons, she speculated that they might want to adopt a daughter. She guessed that when they had the second son, a bit of a risk even in earlier lax times, they were hoping for a girl. If she gave birth to a girl, she decided she would send the infant to their doorstep, hoping they would take her in and adopt her. If they did not know where the child came from, Wanru reasoned, they could not be forced to give her up and return her, even if they were later discovered by local officials. Thus within hours of giving birth to a girl, she asked her husband's brother to take the child there and place her at the family's gate. It was a cold winter's night and the child could not be safely left outside, even wrapped in a warm quilt, so her brother-in-law set off firecrackers and watched nearby to make sure someone came to the door and took the baby inside quickly. Her brother-in-law returned with the news that the infant had been taken in immediately, and they soon heard that the family kept her as predicted. Wanru was sad but resolved that she had done the right thing; the child would be wanted and well cared for in her new family. Without ever approaching the adoptive family, she heard through mutual relatives that the child was doing well and the family was happy to have a daughter. This put her mind at ease.

However, when the girl was about four, a fierce birth planning campaign hit the area where her birth daughter lived. The adoptive family was visited many times by birth planning officials who discovered the girl had been adopted in violation of birth planning regulations. They wanted her returned to the place she came from in order to rid their area of an illegal overquota child. The adoptive family told the officials they had found her at their door and did not know who the birth parents were so they could not return her. However, the officials persisted. So within a few days, the adoptive mother showed up at Wanru's house. She said to Wanru, "If you are the person who left your child at my door and if you want her back, you must take her now. If you do not claim her now, you can never take her back." Without explicitly admitting she was the birth mother, Wanru said, "You have raised this child. She is yours. What decent person would ever interfere in your family and take your daughter from you?" Upon hearing this, the adoptive mother turned and left with no more words spoken. Because they kept the illegally adopted child, the adoptive family was forced to pay a steep fine for an overquota adoption, a child that was also their second overquota child. When Wanru and her husband learned this, they sent money through a third party to help pay the fine because they knew the adoptive family was not rich. The adoptive family did not ask for this help, but Wanru felt it was the right thing to do. She also felt bound by her implicit promise to the adoptive mother not to interfere and stayed away from the family.

However, the adoptive family came again several years later when Wanru's husband was in the hospital dying from liver cancer subsequent to hepatitis B infection. In his final days, the adoptive mother came with her daughter to his hospital room to "pay respects to a distant relative." On her way in, she passed Wanru and, in a low whisper, warned her not to say a word to her daughter. They stayed for a short visit and left. Wanru believed that the adoptive mother felt Wanru's husband should be allowed to see his birth daughter before he died; he gave her life, and this was his last chance to see her. It was a deeply moving, kind, and ethical gesture, Wanru felt, tears filling her eyes. Although these two families barely acknowledged each other, their behavior toward each other was governed by unspoken norms of mutual obligation.

Although by now it was clear that the adopters knew the birth family, aside from certain controlled interactions, the adoptive parents were vigilant about preventing direct contact except on their own limited terms. When the daughter was young, she met her birth brother by accident several times when playing with other children. The word got back to Wanru that the adoptive mother was displeased by this, especially because the boy knew that he had a younger sister who had been "sent to other people." She wanted Wanru to keep the boy away from his birth sister for fear he would figure out who she was.

Yet, when the daughter was getting married, the adoptive mother sent an invitation to Wanru to attend the wedding. Wanru somewhat reluctantly attended, feeling both compelled to do so yet not entirely welcome. She was placed on the edge of the party, where she sat silently with pangs of longing and guilt, but was able to see the bride and her new husband celebrate their marriage. After that time, the adoptive mother told her, "You are her birth mother. Now that she is married, with her own family, you can have a relationship with her, it is up to her to decide." Although from then on, Wanru was free to talk to her daughter, her daughter would not acknowledge her. Wanru can understand how the girl resents her, and probably feels "you didn't want me, now I do not want you." On the other hand, the daughter remains very close to her adoptive mother and father and goes to see them often since her marriage. When we met Wanru in 2009, the recently married daughter was pregnant and soon would have her own child.

Wanru was living alone; her twenty-four-year-old son, following in the footsteps of his deceased father, was in the army, living in Chongqing. She told us she has lots of friends around her and her son calls every week. At fifty years old, she was gregarious and energetic. Yet she was wistful when she spoke of how close her birth daughter was to her adoptive mother, sharing her life and her pregnancy with the mother who raised her and refusing to speak to the mother who gave birth to her. When people speak of why they want a daughter, they usually comment that "daughters are close to their parents, especially their mothers." Although Wanru accepts the choices she has made in her life and says she is not unhappy, she is very aware of what she lost. Standing alone on the outside, she at least knows that she found a good family for her daughter, one that has loved and cared for her well into her adult years.

Although she had been forced to abandon her daughter the night she was born, Wanru was fortunate to know where her daughter was and to watch her from afar, even crossing paths from time to time. We met other birth parents who managed to keep an eye on their daughter at a distance. This always seemed to provide some peace of mind.

Abandoning at a Family Gate #2: Finding a Childless Family (1991)

Birth mother Sun Xiaohua (b. 1965)
Birth father/husband (b. 1966)
First child, girl born 1988
Second child, girl born 1991, abandoned at a doorstep
Third child, boy born 1994

When twenty-six-year-old villager Sun Xiaohua[6] was pregnant with her second daughter in 1991, three years after her first daughter was born, her options were more limited than they would have been in the late 1980s due to increased surveillance in her village. Village officials were under pressure from the county to pay more attention to birth permits, making sure that out-of-plan children were not born and that quotas were met. Living in a village with an agricultural hukou, Xiaohua was allowed by the local 1.5-child policy to have a second birth four years after the birth of her first daughter, but if this second child was discovered and registered it would be difficult to ever have another birth. Xiaohua might be sterilized. So as soon as her second girl was born Xiaohua said she felt great pressure from her parents-in-law who were anxious for their first grandson. They did not say anything directly to Xiaohua, but they pointedly did not come to see the child after her birth. Thus she knew their feelings clearly. Xiaohua felt like she had failed the family even though her husband insisted, "A girl is a human being who has come to the world. We should look at her the same as a boy." Despite her husband's words, Xiaohua quietly decided to "send her second daughter to other people" a month after she was born.

To do this, she turned to her mother to find someone who might want to adopt her daughter. It was impossible to do this openly at this time because of the severe penalties involved, both for her family and for an adoptive family. So Xiaohua's mother made discrete inquiries through her networks of friends and relatives to try to find a good family for the baby, someone who would both want and be allowed to adopt her daughter. If her mother failed to find someone appropriate, Xiaohua knew she could take her daughter to the provincial capital city and abandon her in the city but if she did so she would have no control over who picked her up and might have no clues about where the child would finally go. She felt she must be responsible for her daughter and had to be sure that she found a new home safely. By the early 1990s adoption was difficult in this area; she heard if someone already had a child, they would be punished if they adopted another one or the child might be taken from them by officials. Ideally, they wanted to find a couple that was childless.

Fortunately, Xiaohua's mother located a childless family in a mountainous area not too far away but remote enough to be out of the view of local officials in Xiaohua's village. She heard that their living conditions were good enough and that they were responsible people who wanted a child. Being childless, they could be expected to cherish the child and give her all of their attention, Xiaohua thought, trying to comfort herself. So she decided to send her daughter there, a place where she could later look for her and ensure she was OK.

Once she made the decision she acted immediately, the same day, because she was afraid she wouldn't be able to go through with the plan if she delayed. From the moment she decided, she felt her spirit leave her (*xianshi hunpo*). She continued to try to comfort herself with her mother's assurance that this childless couple longed for a child and would pay a lot of attention to her daughter. She decided to write a letter to leave with the child. As she began writing the letter she wept. She wept so hard she could barely see. (As she spoke to us, over a decade later, her tears again started flowing.) Finally, she wrote: "Thank you for adopting my daughter. I give her the name 'SiSi' (the character for "thought"). Please take good care of her. When she grows up if you want to tell her about me, you can show her this letter that I write to her. But if you do not want to tell her, it is up to you. I promise I will never disturb your life or your family."

The letter she wrote to SiSi said: "I am so sorry and deeply apologize to you. I do not want to do this but am forced to. Please forgive me. Your birthday is —— on the agricultural calendar. When you grow up, you must respect your adoptive parents, the parents who have raised you. If your adoptive parents allow you to look for us, we may see each other some day. But if they do not allow you, we will never see each other again. You should follow their wishes."

Xiaohua cried all night as she went through the motions of making arrangements to take her daughter to the mountainous area where the prospective parents lived. She got a vehicle, a small tractor car, from neighbors. As she left the house, her husband grabbed her arm and tried to stop her. In her heart she wanted to listen to him but she argued with him saying, "Look at your parents, how disappointed and uneasy they are. They want a grandson very much and I have given them two granddaughters. How can I bear to send my own child away? It breaks my heart, but I am sending her to somebody who will pay attention to her as their only child and will love her."

With great difficulty Xiaohua then pulled away from him and went with her mother who was holding the child. After a two-hour ride, they arrived in the mountain area. It was already past 10 p.m.

Xiaohua breast-fed the child on the road and wanted to feed her one more time before leaving her, but the baby had fallen asleep and Xiaohua did not want to wake her for this moment of final separation. She and her mother put SiSi in front of the family gate and set off firecrackers to be sure to draw their attention. They had to leave quickly, Xiaohua said, or there could be trouble that would jeopardize the adoption. The family must not catch them or know who they are. If they know who the parents are, not only would Xiaohua and her husband be punished for the out-of-plan birth but local officials might force the family to return the child even if they wanted to keep her.

When Xiaohua returned home in the middle of the night, she cried and cried without stop. Her husband, who had not slept, criticized her, yelling, "I told you not to do this!" He was very angry and upset and kept repeating these words between his tears, until they both finally fell asleep at dawn in a state of exhaustion. Xiaohua said that he was an honest, down-to-earth person who loved his baby and felt trapped and made impotent by what had happened to his family. For a long time both parents grieved. Xiaohua said her husband finally relented and his anger at her dissipated, knowing that she and her mother had done this for the sake of his parents and their family. It could not be undone.

By the time Xiaohua was pregnant for the third time, she heard about the use of ultrasound to determine the sex of the fetus. She thought she could arrange this, but in the end decided she would not seek out the use of ultrasound. They both decided that whether the baby was a boy or girl, they would keep it. They could not bear to abandon another child. By the time this third child was born, her parents-in-law already had a grandson from one of the younger of their four sons. When Xiaohua was pregnant the third time, her mother-in-law said, "I have four sons and one daughter but the sons are of no use. If we have another girl in the family, that will be good." Xiaohua knew that her mother-in-law, having witnessed the distress of her son, also felt guilty about the abandonment of her second granddaughter and later regretted her attitude when the girl was born. Yet, as fate would have it, Xiaohua's third pregnancy proceeded with a birth permission certificate and produced the previously longed-for son.

Despite this ultimate "success," Xiaohua never stopped thinking about her second daughter. Indeed, she says she has thought of the second child almost every day since leaving her. Although it has been difficult, Xiaohua has kept the promise she made in her letter not to contact the adoptive family or try to see her daughter. But she has inquired through others many times and has learned some information. She hears from other people that the girl is very clever, studies hard, and gets good grades in school. Her adoptive parents take good care of her and are proud of her. Xiaohua knows if she goes to inquire herself, the adoptive parents might find out and would be very upset. So she must be content with secondhand reports and watch from afar. Ethically, she believed that the adoptive parents had assumed the burden and hence all the rights of raising her birth child without interference. For this she should respect them and be grateful. She guessed that if her daughter knew the truth, she would never forgive her, the birth mother who sent her away, and would never be willing to call her *mama* even if they ever met. Abandoning a child was seen as irrevocable and in some ways unforgivable.

Xiaohua's first daughter, who was attending the county teachers' college when we met Xiaohua in 2004, has known the story of what happened to her younger sister for many years. Xiaohua says her first daughter is very filial, rarely complaining as other children do about discipline; she even gives her mother massages when she is tired. One wonders what sense of gratitude, guilt, or insecurity the older daughter felt as a result of having her younger sister sent away to make room for her younger brother while she herself was kept.

She says someday she will look for her sister and says if she finds her she will earn money to support her younger sister's education so she can have the opportunities she has had. Although there is some peace in knowing that the abandoned second baby girl is living a normal and apparently happy life as someone else's daughter, the ethical breach of abandonment is felt by the sibling who was kept as well as by the parents.[7]

Overquota Birth Guerrilla Base: Abandoning in a County Town (1992)

Birth mother Wang Nan (b. 1968)
Birth father/husband (b. 1967), worked in county town
First child, girl born 1991
Second child, girl born 1992, abandoned on the street
Third child, girl born 1996

It was usually crucial to parents' peace of mind to know where their child ended up, to know she was safe, and to try to keep track of her life. Wanru and Xiaohua were comforted by this knowledge. Yet many people who abandoned a baby in this era of tightened birth planning never knew exactly what happened to their child. In over half of the nearly 350 cases of abandonment that we learned about, the parents did not know who picked up the child or where she ended up. Wang Nan[7] and her husband were among those who never knew for sure who picked up their daughter or where she was taken.

In 1992 Wang Nan's second daughter was born secretly outside her village in a county town, just one year after the birth of her first daughter. The birth was illegal. Birth planning was tight in their village at this time and, although Wang Nan was entitled to another birth because her first was a girl, she was required to wait four years by local regulations, so this pregnancy was out of plan. If they stayed in their village, Wang Nan would be forced to abort. Her husband, who was doing business in the county town, found out that there was a *chaosheng youji dui* (超生游击队) area in the town—an "overquota birth guerrilla base area"—an area where one could secretly rent a space to live outside the view of local officials. Others had done it and gotten away with it. Apparently, the town officials paid no attention to those from outside. So they decided to move to the county town and rent a house to hide Wang Nan's pregnancy. When Wang Nan gave birth to another girl, they decided they had to hide her birth to avoid being sterilized, as required after a second birth by local rules at that time, especially after an illegal out-of-plan birth such as this one. Although they would have accepted a large fine, sterilization was unacceptable.

Although Wang Nan claimed she did not care that much about having a son for herself, she felt great pressure from others. Her mother-in-law was a widow, and although she didn't say anything, Wang Nan knew she wanted a grandson. Her husband also felt he needed a son; it was his obligation to his mother and deceased father as well as something they thought they needed for their own economic security or in case of illness. With no social safety net in the countryside, they believed they faced destitution in old age without an adult son. Wang Nan also felt great social pressure. She said repeatedly, "You don't know how important it is to people in the countryside to have a boy. To rural people this is a very heavy matter. You can't imagine the pressure. I do not care for myself, but it is hard to ignore others." It seemed as if her worth as a daughter-in-law, wife and village member hinged on this one matter.

So a few days after the birth of their out-of-plan second daughter, the couple together made the difficult decision to "send the baby to other people." Early in the morning, they wrapped the baby in a quilt with some clothes, milk powder, and 20 yuan. Wang Nan's husband took the child and walked a few minutes from the house they rented. He placed the baby in a cart attached to a small truck parked on the road and then backed into an area just out of sight to watch, moving away from time to time to avoid looking suspicious. Unfortunately, while he was away for a brief time, the baby disappeared. Apparently, someone took the baby and left. Upset and anxious, he asked around the area to see if anyone had seen who took the baby. Someone told him they had seen a couple they recognized take the child. They said this was a childless couple with a "double salary," meaning they both had salaried state jobs. This was an ideal family to take the baby. This was the story the husband told Wang Nan when he returned. When he told her, she cried because she was sad someone had taken her baby and also because she was relieved that apparently a suitable couple had picked up the baby. Yet there was lingering uncertainty because her husband had failed to see clearly what happened. This uncertainty remained twelve years later when we met Wang Nan. While she thought she had some clues as to who had adopted her child, she did not know for sure, something that still haunted her even though she tried to believe the best.

After the birth of her second daughter, Wang Nan had an IUD inserted to avoid another out-of-plan pregnancy. She removed it three years later when she was finally given permission to give birth again, four years after the officially recorded birth of her first daughter, the only birth that the local authorities knew about. This time they lived in their home village in the countryside throughout the pregnancy. They had permission to give birth this time, so she was not compelled to hide the pregnancy. When this third birth was another girl, a neighbor told her she knew some "good people" who were looking for a girl to adopt, and they could secretly send the child to them and immediately get pregnant again under the same birth permission certificate, a tactic used by some to squeeze two births into one certificate without being noticed. But Wang Nan and her husband decided against the idea of sending away another daughter, even if they could arrange it safely and know who the adoptive parents were. Because this was a legal child, born with a certificate of permission, they would not face ruinous fines as they would have for their second daughter who was an illegal out-of-plan birth, and they could get her a hukou as soon as they reported her birth. Furthermore, unlike the situation in 1991 when birth planning was very tight, local birth planning was more relaxed, and they might even avoid being sterilized after a second legal birth.

Social attitudes were also changing, including their own, and the social pressures to have a son were weakening. Wang Nan's mother-in-law even came to her before the birth and said, "You young people decide according to your wishes." Although she wanted a grandson, she knew the choice to abandon the second daughter had been hard, and she did not want to lose another grandchild.

Above all, the painful experience of abandoning their second daughter left them both feeling they definitely wanted to keep this daughter. Wang Nan imagined that her second daughter would hate her if they ever met. "How could she ever understand the pressure I felt?" Her first daughter, who learned from grandma that her first *meimei* (little sister) was "sent away," often asked her parents, "Why did you give *meimei* away?" They had no answer; it wasn't easy to explain to the daughter they kept what they had done. A few years later Wang Nan could hardly explain it to herself. She had changed, even the village had changed.

Wang Nan commented that in the future she might try to find her second daughter. But all she had to go on were vague rumors. She heard that the family who might have adopted their daughter had moved out of the county, perhaps to avoid being found by their daughter's birth parents and to keep secret from others that their daughter was adopted. We talked to some adoptive parents who took this extraordinary step to keep an adoption secret. If true, this would make it harder than ever to find her.

In the meantime, Wang Nan was busy raising her two daughters and tried not to regret the past too much. In 2004 when we met Wang Nan, birth planning was very tight again, and it seemed unlikely she and her husband would ever have another chance for the son they once longed for, if indeed they would even want to try again.

Abandoning in the City: Fifteen Years of Sorrow and Regret

Birth mother Wang Xiaolan
Husband / birth father
First child, daughter born 1992
Second child, daughter born 1993, abandoned in the city
Third child, son born 2000

Abandoning a child in a public place in a big city was seen by many as a last resort, a step taken when one could not figure out a better and safer solution for hiding the birth of an out-of-plan child. When I began this study, urban state orphanage workers told me that babies abandoned in the city were fortunate because they would be quickly found and taken to the orphanages, whereas those abandoned in the countryside were likely to be left to die. From our research among rural parents we learned a very different story. While the big city was safely anonymous and would not implicate one's local area as the source of the illegal birth, as Xiaohua suggested, abandoning a child in an unknown urban public place left the parent without control over who picked up the child and possibly no idea about what happened to the child afterward, even whether she survived. The city was seen as full of potential physical dangers for an unattended infant and the risk she could fall into the hands of bad people. Indeed, one of the most emotionally burdened birth mothers we spoke to was forced to resort to an anonymous urban abandonment, an act that did not go as she hoped.

Wang Xiaolan[8] was the oldest of five girls. Her father, a respected top village official for more than two decades, was an only son, so it seemed particularly tragic that he had no son to continue his father's family. The only chance to avoid bringing an end to his father's line, according to custom, was to have a grandson take his surname and become the family's male heir. Thus the burden of continuing the family fell on Xiaolan and her sisters, who had to produce a male heir in the next generation.

By the time Xiaolan was pregnant with her first child in 1992, two of her sisters had married and already given birth to two girls each, filling their quotas of permitted births. Their father was getting old, and still there was no grandson. So Xiaolan felt enormous pressure to have a son within her allowed quota, a child who might serve as the heir for two families, her father's and her husband's. Adding to the pressure she felt, her husband's parents also had no grandson yet. So when her first pregnancy produced a girl in late 1992, she waited only a few months before secretly getting pregnant again. She did not yet have permission for a second birth, so she had to hide the pregnancy, staying inside when she began to look pregnant in the spring of 1993. Throughout her pregnancy she was nervous about getting caught and about failing again to produce the son so many people longed for. Because of strict birth limits, every pregnancy was a source of high anxiety. As the eldest daughter, she felt a particularly strong obligation to her beloved father, now a widower, to put him at ease in the last years of his life by giving him a grandson.

In the final tense days before she gave birth a decision was made by her, her husband, and his parents that if this child was another girl they would hide her by "sending her away to other people" so Xiaolan could try again to have a son in a couple of years. Since this second birth was out of plan, she would likely come under pressure to be sterilized if the birth was discovered, something she was will-

ing to submit to only if she succeeded in producing her families'
first son. Adding to the pressure to hide the birth was her father's
reputation as a village leader. His family could not be seen violating
birth planning; they were supposed to be exemplary.

So when Xiaolan again gave birth to a girl, there seemed no
other way but to find a safe place to leave the child secretly far outside of the village area for others to adopt her. At the moment of
birth, Xiaolan's heart sunk in her chest at the realization she had
failed again to produce a son. Profoundly depressed, unable to look
at the newborn, she nonetheless insisted on holding the child and
breast-feeding her; she felt that the child needed to be fed for at least
a day or two so she would be strong enough to survive. Her husband and in-laws worried that her determination would waver if she
held the child too long. They were right. When she finally looked
at her child, she saw that "she was perfect, with a beautiful face and
tiny fingers that grasped [her] hand." Indeed, within hours Xiaolan
felt she could not bear to let this child go and wanted to keep her.
Had it not been for the heavy-handed pressure from her in-laws, as
her husband stood by silently, and her own deep physical and emotional fatigue, she said she would have kept the child regardless of
the consequences. As she wept, they pried the child from her arms
and took her away. Before leaving, she made them wait while she
quickly wrote a note to put in the child's quilt. The note had her
birth date according to the lunar calendar and said the child was
healthy and there were no known family diseases. Through her tears,
she also wrote, "We wanted to keep this child but could not raise her
because of the birth planning policy. We hope a kindhearted person
will adopt her and love her."

As her parents-in-law left with her baby, she made them promise
they would not leave the child until they saw she was safely picked
up and where she was taken. They planned to leave her near a police station, a safe place for either a passerby or the police to find

her quickly. She needed to know the baby was safe, and perhaps she could even know of her whereabouts in the future. She wanted as many clues as possible. Feeling unease, as soon as her parents-in-law left she urged her youngest sister to follow them and make sure they did as they promised. For the next hours she remembers only her tears as she waited for them to return with news of what happened, to hear that the baby was safe. In fact, the plan did not go as promised. The parents-in-law said they took the child into the capital city about two hours away and put her down in a safe area just across the street from a police station, as planned. They waited for a short while but were frightened they would be seen and therefore left before the child was picked up. Xiaolan's sister had lost their trail on the way into the city, so she too returned without any news of what happened to the baby. It was already nearly unbearable that Xiaolan had lost her baby; now the loss was made even more excruciating because she would never know with any certainty that the child was safe. For weeks, Xiaolan could barely speak. She felt both guilt and rage at her in-laws and her husband, her heart was broken, her "spirit left her."

Over time she began to function again, but a sadness fell upon her that was still there when we spoke to her three years later. She offered to tell us the story, then wept the entire time as she recounted it, almost compulsively as if saying the words out loud would diminish their hold on her. At the end she said the local government never found out about the second birth and that she had recently been given permission for another birth, four years after the birth of her first and only recorded daughter. However, after the trauma of abandoning her second daughter, she told us she might not ever have another child. Her husband, sitting silently next to her, interjected quietly that this was a bad idea, but she defiantly persisted saying, "I haven't decided yet. I may never have another child." She added, "If I do decide to have another child, it will not matter whether it is a

girl or a boy. I will keep that child. I will never do this again. Ever."
She continued to worry about what happened to her abandoned
baby, repeating several times that her parents-in-law did not wait
to see what happened as they promised. The accusation was clear
even if unspoken. Their failure weighed heavily on her, as did her
own remorse.

In 2010, we visited Xiaolan again. Her youngest sister, Wulan,
was there as was Xiaolan's husband. Xiaolan seemed much older
than a woman in her mid-forties and seemed worn out, even as she
engaged in small talk with her sister and her visitors. The family
had done well economically and had recently moved into the city,
where her husband worked as an interior decorator. Their fourth-
floor apartment in a ten-year-old building was clean, roomy, newly
painted but spartan, having just moved there from their old village
home that we visited in 1996. They finally had another child in
2000, four years after obtaining permission; this child was the son
for whom so much had been sacrificed. When we were there, their
ten-year-old son was in his room doing homework. My colleague,
who had visited the family several times over the years, told me
that each time they got close to the subject of her second daughter, Xiaolan would weep. Her father asked that the subject not be
broached, telling us that time had not healed her wounds, nor had
the "success" of bearing a son erased her pain. We did not mention
the missing child, although she seemed to hang in the air.

I left early with the younger sister Wulan. She had married when
she finished graduate school and had a son in 2003, their father's
second grandson. They too now lived in the city, where she had a
good job in a company. It ran through my mind that the loss Xiaolan
had suffered in order to give her father an heir had turned out to be
unnecessary, perhaps adding one more layer of pain and regret for
Xiaolan. As we walked down the street, Wulan told me that she had
recently seen a girl on local TV who had been abandoned at birth

and adopted by a local woman, a street cleaner, who found her on the street, perhaps near the area where her niece had been left. The girl looked vaguely like their family and was born in 1993. Wulan located the teenage girl and asked her if her birthday was the date on the note left with her niece; the girl said nothing and quickly shook her head because she did not want her mother to hear her talking to a stranger. But perhaps, Wulan later speculated, the adoptive mother who found her never showed her the note. The woman now seemed very concerned that so many people were coming to inquire about the girl she had raised for seventeen years. The Wang sisters followed other leads over the years, but none led anywhere. Given where the child was left, in a capital city with a state orphanage that did hundreds of international adoptions per year in the 1990s, it was even possible that Xiaolan's daughter ended up in the United States, Canada, or Europe. Wulan confirmed that her sister continues to long for knowledge about her daughter. Wulan says she assumes that if Xiaolan's daughter is alive somewhere, she would hate her birth mother for sending her away. How could a child ever understand, much less forgive, what had happened in those years? At a recent meeting, Xiaolan told me if she ever found her daughter, she hoped not to disturb her life but just wanted to know she was alright and to have a chance to apologize, to tell her how sorry she is for allowing her to be sent away. She told us quietly, "I just want to know that my daughter is alive somewhere in this world. Then my heart can rest." For Xiaolan, an act of abandonment in the 1990s has cast a long shadow indeed. The missing daughter has left a permanent hole in her heart and in the family.

None of the women we spoke to walked away unscarred by what they had done. Even Huang Mei, who had arranged an open adoption among close relatives for her daughter, experienced an uncomfortable breach in the relationship that reflected some sense of betrayal. But those who suffered the most were the parents who never knew for sure where their daughters were or, as in the case of Xiaolan, whether the daughter was even "alive somewhere in this world." Across China, there are tens of thousands of women and men who live with these scars, a rarely acknowledged, largely undocumented cost of China's population policies. Untold numbers of people who were forced to abandon a child in order to hide a birth ache to at least know that their child is OK. Although the adoption literature, like many of our interviews, focuses on birth mothers, many birth fathers also expressed a sense of great loss and shame for not being able to raise their own children. None of the fathers we met appeared as patriarchs who easily and willingly gave up "unvalued" daughters in the pursuit of a male heir. Many fathers we got to know were even more unwilling than mothers to lose a child and appeared humiliated if not broken by being unable to raise their own children. Most parents we talked to felt that they were coerced by policies and circumstances, that they had "no choice"; yet at the same time they bore the heavy burden of being made complicit in an act that violated the ethical obligations that parents have toward children, an act that broke bonds of parental love that should have held. The emotional consequences of coercion and complicity, loss and guilt follow some people for many years. As we will see later, even those who literally had no choice, not even a "coerced choice," whose child was seized from their unwilling arms by government officials, felt a painful mix of excruciating loss and personal failure. Perhaps the sense of complicity and failure explains why birth parents who often expressed anger at themselves and other family members did not overtly express anger at the government policies and officials they felt trapped them. In contrast, adoptive parents who struggled with government policies were more likely to express anger, even rage, at those policies and officials, as we will see later.

We did not talk in depth to many of the abandoned children who were adopted locally, but we met some of them when interviewing the adoptive parents who found them and raised them, the subject of the next chapter. When we started this project, these children were either too young or, in about half the cases, were unaware that they had been adopted. As we followed up on families we met at the beginning of our research, the earliest cohort of abandoned children have become young adults, and we have learned more about their feelings and attitudes toward their birth parents as well as their adoptive families. Although the handful of adopted daughters that we have talked to expressed a variety of attitudes toward birth parents, they most often expressed resentment, anger, or simple disregard for the birth parents who abandoned them or sent them away, just as Xiaolan and other relinquishing birth parents imagine. As we will discuss later, even children who were only sent away to be hidden temporarily with friends and relatives may express resentment toward parents or other family members. Some abandoned adopted children declare that they hate their birth parents, whether they are known or unknown to them. This is especially true for those who have been told that they were left alone in a public place. Rejecting birth parents is for some an expression of loyalty to their "real parents," the parents who raised them. The expression we often heard from adults—"The parent who raises the child has greater weight than the one who gives birth"—reflects the attitudes we heard from the older children. Many credit their adoptive parents with "saving" them. In our research, these "real parents" who welcomed the abandoned daughters of strangers into their families were more numerous than we originally imagined given the tight legal restrictions and penalties against unofficial adoption. As we will see, some adoptive parents did indeed save the abandoned daughters of strangers from circumstances that risked their fragile lives and paid a price for doing so.

CHAPTER 3

Adopting Daughters and Hiding Out-of-Plan Children

Our original interest in Chinese adoption was spurred by the rise of international adoption of abandoned children from Chinese orphanages in the 1990s. As discussed in the first chapter, the dominant discourse of those involved in these adoptions, reinforced by officials and agencies in both China and the receiving countries (primarily the United States and Canada), was that these abandoned children, mostly girls, could not find adoptive homes in China due to the strong patriarchal cultural preference for sons and the general lack of acceptance of adoption outside of one's own bloodlines. International adopters were assured by US adoption agencies and media accounts that nobody in China wanted these discarded girls of unknown parentage, or at least not enough to deal with the deluge of abandoned Chinese girls that filled some state orphanages. What our research uncovered, on the contrary, was that the overcrowding of orphanages and creation of a pool of children available for international adoption was closely related to, if not wholly caused by, active government suppression of customary adoption practices, limiting their numbers and pushing many more into the shadows along with the out-of-plan children who were involved in these adoptions.

Even before we began our study of abandonment and adoption we knew from the demographic study of Sten Johansson and Ola Nygren, published in 1991, that "informal adoptions" had apparently increased significantly in the 1980s, amounting to several hundreds of thousands annually, and that these adoptions increasingly involved girls.[1] Demographers had noticed by the late 1980s that the reported sex ratios at birth had become unnaturally and increasingly skewed in favor of boys over the decade, leading to speculation about what was happening to the girls who should have been born. Johansson and Nygren argued that informal unregistered adoption was one place where the so-called missing girls disappeared.

We wondered what these "informal adoptions" looked like and how they compared to past patterns of adoptions in China. Were these temporary arrangements among relatives and friends merely for the purpose of deceiving authorities, or were they actual adoptions of children into other people's families? Did they involve abandoned children? Or were they adoptions arranged among relatives? We did in fact find various arrangements for temporarily hiding children that masqueraded as "adoption" but were merely a means to hide a child's true identity. Generally, these were transparent to the participants and not considered to fall into the category of actual adoptions. Most of the real adoptions we found were permanent arrangements that fully incorporated children into the family, usually "as if the adopted child was a birth child," that is, assuming the status, rights, and responsibilities of birth children in the family. Most of these adoptions were "informal" only in the sense that they were often unregistered. The term "de facto adoption" or "actual adoption" (*shishi shouyang* 事实收养)—a term that is frequently used to designate unregistered adoptions that occur outside government channels and knowledge—is a better term than "informal," because the latter term implies a fluidity of relationships or a tentative commitment of parents that did not generally characterize the majority of adoptions we studied.[2] These were "strong adoptions," also known as plenary adoptions in the comparative adoption literature, similar to US adoption practices.

We found that in the 1990s and early 2000s, as international adoption grew from a few hundred a year to a peak of fourteen thousand in 2005,[3] many people in China were adopting healthy abandoned or otherwise relinquished female children to raise "as if their own" and that they did so despite the legal restrictions and birth planning punishments that could be, and often were, imposed on local adopters. It is possible that only a minority of healthy abandoned children in this area made it through the social net of local adopters into the hands of orphanages, saving these generally underfunded and understaffed institutions from more severe overcrowding than they experienced in the 1990s. By 2007, when abandonment had clearly declined in the main area of our research, the head of a large state orphanage commented that they no longer received more than a few healthy infants in a year, not only because abandonment was down, but also because under reduced age restrictions (from thirty-five to thirty) and relaxed registration procedures, the surrounding population could adopt legally more easily than in the past and consequently almost all of the remaining abandoned healthy babies were adopted before they ever reached the orphanage, leaving mostly disabled abandoned infants for the orphanage. Of our sample of over one thousand adoptive families, primarily from the same south central region, more than half were adoptions of abandoned infants of unknown parents and over 90 percent of those were girls. Most of these adoptions, probably like the majority in China, were unregistered de facto adoptions, numbering annually in the hundreds of thousands.[4] Only a handful of the adoptive parents we interviewed met the legal requirements for adoption specified in the 1991 adoption law, which required that adopters be childless and over thirty-five (later lowered to thirty); the adoptive parents were either too young or they had other children at the time of adoption. Thus, to the extent that local officials followed the law, registered adoption was not an option for most. Parents for their part had little reason to register an adoption except to obtain a hukou in their household for their child, something that an illegally adopted child was not entitled to. As we will see, the inability to obtain a hukou was, and continues to be, a persistent problem for adopted children and their families except for the minority who are adopted officially from state orphanages. As we discovered, it was often easier and no more costly to register the child as one's own out-of-plan birth child.

On the other hand, we also discovered many fake or on-paper-only "adoptions" and other informal arrangements undertaken wholly as a means of hiding a child and disguising its true identity. People generally distinguished these fake adoptions or temporary fostering arrangements from real or actual adoptions. Ironically, unlike many actual or de facto adoptions, fake adoptions were sometimes legally registered as if they were real adoptions and hence conferred an overtly legal status on the fake-adopted child by providing a hukou and giving the child a legal existence, in effect citizenship, in the residential area of the fake adoptive parents. These fake adoptions and other informal hiding arrangements do not appear in our survey of adoptive families; rather we learned about these patterns of hiding children when asking parents about *heihaizi*—"black children" or hidden children. These patterns will be discussed below at the end of this chapter.

First, we will turn our attention to the group of adoptive parents we interviewed in depth. Although there has been a lot of media attention paid to the over 120,000 Chinese children adopted by North American and European families, hundreds of thousands of adoptive Chinese parents of this same cohort of children have remained invisible to the international adoption community and neglected by most research on adoption.[5] The purpose here is to fill in this void.

Portraits of Adoption

A "FOREVER FAMILY" FOR AN OVERQUOTA DAUGHTER (1987)

Wu Dazhu, adoptive father (b. 1960)
Tian Liya, adoptive mother (b. 1960)
First child, son born 1982
Second child, son born 1984
Third child, daughter (Wu Biyun) adopted 1987

Wu Biyun[6] was an overquota daughter adopted within days of her birth in 1987 by friends of her birth parents who had two sons and wanted a daughter. Although adoptions in the 1990s increasingly involved "abandoned" children as birth planning authorities cracked down on arranged adoptions as a means of circulating and hiding out-of-plan children, in the 1980s adoptions directly arranged between families, such as Biyun's, were common and growing in number. In this area this kind of arranged adoption was an extension of customary practices among networks of *qin-you* (friends and relatives) that grew more popular in the early 1980s in the wake of the first birth planning campaigns. Biyun's birth mother and adoptive mother migrated together to south central China from the same village in Sichuan. Biyun was the third child, all girls, born to her birth parents. While birth planning was not intense in their village when Biyun was born, several overquota children were already a liability and brought fines and pressure from local officials to stop bearing children. Biyun's birth parents wanted to keep trying to have a son, so they decided to hide Biyun's birth by adopting her out to friends in another village. Biyun's adoptive family had two young sons and wanted a daughter, especially her adoptive father, the youngest of three brothers in a large extended family still residing in the same village with their wives and children. Having children of each gender was considered ideal, they said.

There were several adoptions scattered throughout this extended, multigenerational family, representing different kinds of adoption practices over the years. The eldest brother, Wu Dage, born in the mid-1930s, was married to a woman who was taken in by his parents as a "little foster daughter-in-law" (*tongyangxi*), the term for a girl usually adopted as an infant or toddler who at maturity was intended to marry one's son. This is a practice that was never very widespread in this area and, by all accounts, had almost vanished in the 1950s.[7] Dage's spouse was an unusual case. She was the daughter of family friends who died when she was eight and was adopted into the Wu family primarily because she was homeless. So she did not truly fit the "foster daughter-in-law" tradition. But a poor family with three sons would have a hard time affording to marry so many sons. Having the adopted girl marry their oldest son was a way to reduce this financial burden, sparing them the costs of a betrothal, wedding ceremony, and customary bride price. When we met the couple in 1996, their only daughter, whom they also adopted as an infant,[8] was twenty-eight and was married with a daughter and son by birth.

Wu Dagui, the second brother, was a local schoolteacher married to a woman who had been adopted as an infant by a childless couple in a nearby village. Dagui's wife's adoptive mother, now a widow, lived with them and their two teenage children, a boy and a girl, who called her Lao Lao (maternal grandmother). According to dominant patrilineal traditions, it was an unusual arrangement for the wife's mother to move into the family of her daughter's husband. But Dagui explained that his mother-in-law was a widow with no other children. When an adopted daughter was an only child, she and her husband were expected to provide care for her elderly parents. Lao Lao and her adopted daughter had always been very close, and Lao Lao would spend the rest of her life in their household. Lao Lao was a gregarious character who totally dominated the room when she was present. Living a life outside the normative ideal seemed only to have sharpened her tongue, wit, and interpersonal skills, and taught her how to command others' attention and compliance, be they teenage grandchildren or family guests.

Wu Dazhu was the youngest brother, twenty years younger than Dage, the oldest. He had wanted a daughter ever since the birth of his first son in 1982. So despite the threat of birth planning fines, he and his wife Tian Liya had a second child in 1984, a violation that cost them all of their furniture and their front door because they did not have any money to pay the fine for the overquota birth. Unfortunately for Dazhu's hopes for a daughter, this child was also a son. A few years later, Biyun's birth parents approached Wu Dazhu and Tian Liya to see if they wanted to adopt their newborn third daughter. Dazhu was immediately happy at the prospect, and although Tian Liya had some reservations about rearing a third child, as well as having to pay another fine or lose more furniture, they both agreed to the adoption. Years later, Liya laughed when we asked about the penalty for adopting Biyun, remembering that this time they paid several hundred yuan, quite a sum for them at the time, and lost their table. It seemed they could have furniture or children but not both at the same time. In fact, they hardly had room for furniture anyway. With three young children and only farming work to rely on, they were the poorest of the three Wu families and lived in one of the most rundown houses in the village—three small dark rooms, one filled with farm tools, straw, and bags of rice, with a low thatched roof and a rough, uneven dirt floor. A small unventilated stove polluted the inside air and made it hard to breath. To ease pressure at home, the oldest son lived some of the time with Wu Dage

and his wife, serving as a kind of surrogate adoptive son to his older
uncle now that Dage's only daughter had married and moved away
into her in-law's family with her husband, in the typical patrilineal,
patrilocal fashion.

Biyun, as the "baby" in this extended family, grew up to be a
feisty child who sometimes tried her overworked mother's patience
and provoked frequent scoldings. When her mother got really angry with her, she reportedly raised the specter of returning Biyun
to her birth family, saying to her daughter, "If you don't behave I
will send you back to your birth mother!" Biyun would yell back,
"You are my mother. This is my family. You can't send me back." In
these fights Biyun turned to her father who assured her she was their
daughter forever and would not be sent back. Biyun also spent time
with Lao Lao, who lived just across the lane at Uncle Dagui's house.
Lao Lao seemed more patient with the child's temper, and they got
along well.

When occasionally Biyun went to visit her birth family, she did
not like staying there. She did not feel close to her sisters or to the
younger brother who was finally born after the birth of a fourth girl
who, unlike Biyun, stayed with the family because "birth planning
was loose" in their village the year she was born. It seemed likely that
Biyun resented being sent away while her numerous siblings stayed
with her birth parents. Like all of the adopted children we learned
about in arranged and open adoptions, she preferred and showed
loyalty to her adoptive family. Yet she seemed to feel as if she didn't
entirely belong to either family, although as she grew older, she and
her adoptive mother got along better. She barely finished junior
middle school before she quit school to earn money to help her
parents who were saving for their sons' future marriages. Although
Biyun said her reason for quitting was to help her parents, in fact
she hated studying and did poorly; she was bored in school and was
constantly criticized by her teachers for her bad performance and

inability to concentrate. Although her parents urged her to stay in school, she finally refused.

The family's poverty, exacerbated by birth planning fines and confiscations as well as the burden of three young children, led her mother years later to remark somewhat wistfully that raising three children was too great a burden and that the "modern" preference for smaller families that had become prevalent in this area by the late 1990s was definitely more desirable. Yet it was not the burden of Biyun that she seemed to lament most at the time, but rather the burden of having two sons. Parents had the financial responsibility to help sons get married and set up a home. With their meager farming income and high agricultural taxes (finally abolished in their village in 2005), it seemed impossible that they could ever save enough money for these obligations. Biyun, on the other hand, started contributing a bit of income when she quit school to go to work, and it would be her future husband's responsibility to build and furnish their house. One boy and one girl would have been ideal, Tian Liya mused. Biyun's birth mother, who joined our conversation one day, concurred. Her long quest for a son had left her exhausted and poor, raising four children, and wondering if it was all worth it. When I visited the women again several years later, they both had converted to protestant Christianity "for the comfort" it brought to their difficult lives. Marking the conversion, Liya had a large Christian poster taped on the wall of a new room they had added to their old house—an image of a cross, which also looks like the Chinese number ten, with the Ten Commandments written below.

The problem of providing housing for the marriage of two sons became a moot point in 2009 when the entire village was abruptly moved to provide land for a high-speed railroad connecting the provincial capital to Beijing, one of the national construction projects the Chinese government initiated during the 2008 global economic recession. All three Wu brothers and their families were moved within months to a new high-rise complex overlooking the area that was once their village. Everyone over the age of eighteen would receive a monthly payment of around 800 yuan to compensate for the loss of land and livelihood. Along with the heavily subsidized new housing, this was enough for a couple to retire; supplemented with another job it allowed a standard of living substantially above the family's previous situation. The youngest son, now married, lived with Wu Dazhu and Tian Liya in their spacious four-bedroom modern apartment along with his wife and newborn son. Biyun, who had unexpectedly married very young and already had a three-year-old daughter when we visited in 2010, was also living in the apartment with her parents as she considered a divorce from her heavy-drinking, abusive husband. She had not done well in recent years, but her feisty nature remained evident. She had married against her parents' wishes and now contemplated a divorce that her mother also felt unwise because of the young child she shared with her husband. The discussion about the divorce inevitably led back to old disputes about quitting school against her mother's advice as she now found herself unemployed without job skills or the means to support herself and her daughter outside the marriage. Although Biyun and her mother still did not see eye to eye on many things, her parental home was a secure refuge from a bad marriage. In recent years, she had lost all contact with her birth family and did not consider them part of her life. It was her adoptive family that provided succor and support to her as a young adult. As her father had told her when she was a young naughty child, "we are your family forever."

Although the family was now financially secure, Wu Dazhu was despondent over the loss of his land and livelihood. Not ready to retire and sit home, he went out every day to find work as a day laborer. He had no skills other than farming, something he said he knew how to do even though he was poor. He said now people look down on him as he hires himself out each day to do menial jobs. After dinner one night when we were visiting, he sat in a corner with an old flute as he often did in the evening. Biyun brought him a book of music notations and sat next to him listening to him play as others carried on conversations. It seemed father and daughter were still close despite the turmoil in her life. We imagined that living with his son, grandson, and daughter provided Dazhu some solace as he found himself caught in the whirlwind of changes that reverberate throughout China. At the same time, the family provided a safe haven for the unemployed daughter whose marriage had failed.

"LEFT FOR DEAD": FINDING A BABY IN A GARBAGE DUMP

Li Rong, adoptive father (b. 1943)
Wan Aiying, adoptive mother (b. 1945)
First child, son born 1971, drown 1986
Second child, daughter born 1987, adopted as a foundling 1987

Wan Aiying and Li Rong,[9] an older couple nearing their sixties, met us in 2004 on a small street several blocks from where they lived in a small picturesque town surrounded by hills and small tea farms. They did not want their neighbors to overhear our conversation. The adoption of their daughter as a foundling in 1987 remained a secret to most people in their neighborhood and, especially, to their then seventeen-year-old daughter who was away at school. An official in the town knows about their family's situation but keeps it secret; virtually no one else knows anything about their daughter's true origins.

They found her by chance only a short time after suffering the unbearable loss of their fifteen-year-old son who accidentally drowned in an uncovered well. Already in their early forties at the time of his death, they were too depressed to think about whether they could have another child. Their grief had hardly eased when one night Li Rong found a newborn infant girl barely alive in a garbage dump. Out unusually late to rent a quilt for a visiting relative, he passed by the garbage dump and noticed a dog rummaging around in a pile of garbage. As he got closer he heard the faint cry of a baby and then saw blood everywhere and a woman's bloody sanitary pad. Amidst the bloody refuse was a tiny, naked infant. Shocked to see this tiny baby gasping and crying, he whisked her into his arms and ran home with her in a panic, fearful that she might die as he held her. At home the gasping and crying calmed as they did their best to feed and care for her, still not sure such a small thing could survive. They fed her a mixture of milk powder, rice gruel, and honey for several days, taking turns staying awake with her to keep her warm and feed her every hour. Li Rong soon went to his boss in the town's forestry bureau and told him about the baby, asking him for advice about how to handle the situation. They had grown attached to this tiny baby and were determined to nurse her to health and keep her. Li Rong's boss told him, "You have no child now, so you should be able to adopt this child. We can help you get permission. This is a good thing for the government. No one will cause you trouble." When he told his wife what his boss said, she was overjoyed to know they could keep the baby.

For several months they nursed and cared for the child around the clock. They visited the doctor many times over the first few months, using all of their savings. It seemed that she was born early, her premature birth perhaps intentionally induced. She was supposed to die, they guessed, a victim of an act of infanticide. But she slowly gained weight and soon began to flourish like a normal baby, becoming stronger and easier to care for. They loved her "as their own." She was the gift they needed to help mend their own broken hearts.

But the procedures necessary to give her a legal status in their family did not go as smoothly as Li Rong's boss suggested. Although he tried to help them, they had to fight for many years to get their daughter a hukou in their family. They had recently moved from their village to the county town after the death of their son. The forestry bureau had made a special effort to help the couple at that time, giving them a new house in town. But getting a county town hukou for the daughter was almost impossible. The police argued that she was an abandoned child and not entitled to a town hukou; she probably came from the countryside, they reasoned. Furthermore, with twisted logic, the police insisted she was their second child, which was not allowed in the county town. But a proper hukou in the county town would be necessary for her to go to school to get an education, so they fought on, spending time and most of their money on the effort. Finally, after several years, several thousand yuan, and the intervention of the forestry bureau, they got her a town hukou, but not before leaving Li Rong with a bitter taste. He said with some anger that he and his wife had saved the government the cost of raising this child yet the government would not even give her a proper hukou. "Perhaps the government would have preferred she had died in the garbage dump," he said with disgust. Li Rong also felt that they were entitled to an "only-child certificate" for her because she was an only child in their family after the death of their son and she deserved the benefits that accrued to that status at the time—a small monthly stipend and reduction of various fees, such as those for inoculations and school fees. There was no way the local government would accede to this request.

When their daughter was four, Li Rong and Aiying were surprised one day when a couple with a six-year-old boy showed up at the house and said they were their adopted daughter's birth parents. They said they did not want to cause trouble or claim their child, they just wanted to be relatives or friends. They explained that they abandoned their daughter because of pressure from birth planning. They were setting up a business in town and waiting to transfer their hukou. They were told they were not allowed to have a second child; if they did so, they would be fined and lose the town hukou and their business. Now several years later, they were well off and wanted to help out with the adoptive family's expenses. As Li Rong and Aiying listened to this story, they became extremely angry. Aiying said, "You tried to kill your baby for your own profit, then you abandoned her because she was not yet dead! The first months after we picked her up we struggled to keep her alive, we stayed up with her all night, taking shifts to take care of her. You knew this and you never came to help. Now you see how lovely she is, so you come to be our 'relatives.' We don't want to be your relatives. We don't want you to come here or to see our daughter." The birth parents came back three or four more times, but each time Li Rong and Aiying sent them away and prevented them from seeing their daughter. Finally, they stopped coming.

When we met, Li Rong and Aiying's daughter was in a special "review school" to prepare for the national university exams. The first time she took the exams she did not do well enough to get into the four-year university she wanted to attend. Her parents were supporting her with all of their savings, even selling their home and moving to a cheaper place in order to raise the money for her education. They had already sold their larger home in town and moved to a smaller one. Next they planned to sell this home and move back to their village where housing and living expenses are very cheap. They told us their daughter is very "filial" and close to them, phoning home several times a week, sometimes tearfully telling them she is homesick and misses them. She frets about her parents sacrificing so much for her education.

To date, her parents had told her nothing about her adoption, although one wonders if she really could be clueless all these years. They had told her many times about the older brother who died before she was born, so this tragedy was part of the known family history. But they never wanted to tell her how they found her and had never thought the time was right for her to know she was not born into her family. Meeting us outside their neighborhood was an extra precaution to keep their story secret, ensuring that no one but them can ever tell her the truth. Approximately half the adoptions we learned about were kept secret from the children, sometimes even when the adoptions were known to friends and relatives, while about half were known to the children involved, sometimes at a relatively young age. There are many reasons for secrecy in adoption and many parties to consider—such as the government, the neighbors, the child. Many adoptions were kept secret from authorities for obvious policy reasons—to avoid fines or the possible seizure of the child. By the 1990s customary adoptions had become a practice fraught with difficulties, one that could bring risk to parents, who could be fined, and the child, who could be taken away from an adoptive family. As a result, unless the adoptive parents met the legal requirements for an adoption, adopted children were often reported as out-of-plan birth children, a ruse that sometimes facilitated registration, although at the expense of a fine and possibly sterilization. There were also other reasons that people might keep adoptions secret—to avoid the shame of infertility; to avoid the social stigma that attaches to adoption as inferior to biological family ties; to avoid hurting the child's feelings and sense of security, and to prevent teasing by others; to protect the parent-child relationship from interference by birth family relationships; to guard against the possibility of "losing the child's love." In our interviews, the desire to avoid hurting or unsettling the child, at least until the child is "old enough to understand," was among the most common reasons given for maintaining secrecy from the child.

Li Rong and Aiying worried most about hurting their daughter's feelings and self-esteem should she learn the truth about her abandonment and adoption. Now that she was old enough to tell her the truth, they were still afraid the shock of it would disturb her peace of mind, disrupt her study, and throw her off track, making her future more difficult. Were they also afraid she might love them less, knowing they were not her biological parents? They insisted they had no fear of this; they had raised her as their own child from the first hours of her life. They were confident of their bond. But what turmoil would it create for her to know her origins, to know that she was thrown away in the garbage? Li Rong believed she deserved the truth, but he didn't want to tell it. He was just beginning to compose a letter to his daughter to explain how she came to be their daughter, although it was hard for him to find the right words. Aware that he and his wife were getting older, he wanted to have the letter ready for his daughter in case they died before telling her. If he proceeded with this plan, it was difficult to imagine what it would be like for her to read this for the first time in the midst of her grief over the loss of a parent that she was so close to. As he thought this through, he realized that he would have to find a way to talk to their daughter before too long. But not now, as she was preparing for her college entrance exams. When would he ever find a good time, he wondered?

FOUND AT THE DOOR: THE GIRL WHO DARED CROSS THE "EVIL GATE" (E-MEN)

Ruan Shouji, mother (b. 1955)
Husband (b.1955)
First child, son born 1979
Second child, son born 1981
Third child, girl born and adopted 1990, abandoned at family's
    door

One night in December 1990, Ruan Shouji[10] was awakened around midnight by the sound of firecrackers in her courtyard. Alarmed, she ran to the door and opened it, quickly noticing a bundled baby right at the door. She immediately understood what had just happened. She picked up the baby, walked out into the dark courtyard, and called into the night, "Who are you? Come out. Please do not leave your baby here. We already have two children and I cannot take care of this third child, it's not allowed. We have no time or money to raise another. Please take her to someone else who can raise her. Come out, I know you are there!" No one emerged, and Shouji had to retreat inside with the baby to escape the cold air. This was the second time someone had left a child at her door. The first time was a year ago. She immediately took that baby to the village government birth planning office; they said abandoned babies had to be sent to the government, who would then take them to the local orphanage. This time she was hesitant to send another baby to the orphanage. Over the next few days she talked to family and neighbors about what to do with this baby. No one knew who had left the child, but it was likely that the birth family knew them. Shouji was a schoolteacher, and her husband was a shopkeeper in town. It would be known that they were an economically stable family who furthermore had two school-age sons and no daughter. From a customary point of view, they were perfect candidates to adopt an infant girl.

She remembers her neighbors urged her to keep the child saying, "You have no daughter, you should keep her. Your sons are in school, so you can handle it. She will bring happiness to your family." When she hesitated, someone else suggested, "Just take her in for a while until you know what you want to do with her." So she kept her for a while and quickly became deeply attached to her. Indeed, the entire family wanted to keep the child, considering it a blessing that this beautiful healthy baby girl had come to their door.

Shouji's mother-in-law was particularly happy to have a girl in the family—at last. Shouji said her mother-in-law was a superstitious woman who believed this family was cursed by an *e-men*, an

evil gate that frightened away all girl babies. It had been three generations since a girl was born into the family. Shouji's husband was
the youngest of three boys, with no sisters. His oldest brother had
three sons and the other had two sons, so between the three brothers
there were seven sons and still no daughters. Now two of the sons
had one son each and were not allowed any more children under the
birth planning rules that were being enforced at the time. Shouji's
mother-in-law thought this girl was very special and very brave to
come to their door, and so she was pleased when they decided to
adopt her. Shouji laughed at her mother-in-law's "superstition." But
indeed they were all happy to welcome this child into the family. So
despite her nervousness about a third child, Shouji and her husband
decided to raise her as their daughter. She quickly became the whole
family's favored little niece and baby sister.

Although many parents keep adoptions secret from their children until they are older, even when neighbors or family members
know, when Shouji's daughter was barely five years old she decided
to tell her she was adopted. Shouji had already overheard some children tell her daughter that she did not really "belong" to this family.
Shouji did not want the child to worry about what this meant, so
as soon as she had a chance she told her the truth. The child started
to cry and pounded on her mother with her little fists, saying "No!
No! Don't say that!" Shouji held her and said, "It doesn't matter.
You are the same to me as your brothers. You belong to this family
just like them." A few days later, the child came to Shouji and said,
"Mama, it doesn't matter. You are the same to me as my real mother."
Shouji smiled as she recalled this touching exchange with her young
daughter.

Using their "connections," the family eventually obtained a
hukou for their daughter, taking advantage of the lowered fines
offered around the time of the census, when the government often tries to get families to register "black children." Like most de

facto adoptive families, especially those that do not fit the legal requirements of childlessness, Shouji and her husband never registered the adoption. "Why would we? We got her a hukou as our birth daughter." Many adoptive families found ways to get hukou without ever registering or even acknowledging an adoption. In this area, the fines for an overquota birth and an "overquota adoption" were the same, but the process for getting a hukou for an adopted child, especially one that was "overquota," could be impossible even if the fine was paid. One might even risk having the child seized by drawing official attention to it, as we learned from several adoptive families who lost children. Only a childless couple over thirty-five years might find registering an adoption to be a useful, and perhaps necessary, path to a hukou. In light of our findings, it was not surprising that only a small minority of adoptions were ever registered as such. While some adopted children lived without hukou into adulthood, Shouji's adopted daughter became a legally registered member of her family as an overquota birth child by the time she needed a hukou to go to middle school.

By all accounts, Shouji and her daughter have had a very close relationship (*tie xin*) over the years. As a young adult, the daughter was following in her mother's footsteps, attending a teachers college so she could become a schoolteacher. Shouji was noticeably proud of her and looked forward to her school vacations at home.

Shouji still did not have any idea who her daughter's birth parents were. She said she would not be surprised if they have come around to see their daughter, maybe even spoken to her without identifying themselves. She guessed they might secretly show up at her daughter's wedding in a few years. She said that this would be OK with her, expressing the same view that the adoptive parents of Wanru's daughter expressed. Her daughter could decide about whether or not she wanted a relationship with them as an adult. Unlike some adoptive parents, Shouji and her husband had never

spoken ill of the birth parents who carefully left their infant daughter at their front gate. Nonetheless, from our discussions with other
adoptees who found themselves in this situation, the reception from
the daughter, if the birth parents ever emerge, was likely to be frosty.

Bachelor Fathers — "Bare Branches" and Foundling Daughters

While abandoning parents frequently targeted the doorsteps of
childless and daughterless couples because they were prime candidates to adopt an infant daughter, bachelors were another category
of persons likely to want to adopt a child, albeit one considered far
less ideal.

Adoption provides one "solution" for the bachelor's predica-
ment of being family-less in a society that is still built around patrilineal family and kinship, at least in the countryside. Historically
men without family or the prospects of progeny were misfits, "bare
branches" who brought their family line, their "branch" of the patrilineal family, to an end, a tragedy and disgrace. In times of social and
political disruption, such as the nineteenth and early twentieth century, these men were seen as a recruiting ground for bandit gangs,
warlords, and revolutionary armies. In recent years the "problem"
of bachelors has reemerged in scholarly and political discourse as a
result of the increasingly skewed sex ratios that have accompanied
population control policies in the last three decades. What will happen to the excess men who cannot find wives in the next decades,
the "bare branches" of the twenty-first century? Likely to be more
numerous among the poor, as in the past, the prospect of large numbers of bachelors has raised concerns for political stability, even concerns for war and peace in the minds of some.[11] Alternatively, this
group may be seen as among those "left behind" by the larger changes
of this era, a group that struggles against prejudice and inequality
to build a "normal" life in a society that looks down upon them.[12]

In our sample of nearly one thousand adoptive families, twenty-five were bachelors and seven were single women, all childless widows. The adoption law does not require that adopters be married, although a single man must be forty years older than a female adoptee. Single women have no additional restriction, although in practice single women who have never been married may be denied the right to adopt because they cannot guarantee future childlessness unless they are past childbearing age. Bachelors might also have trouble adopting from orphanages because they are not considered ideal adoptive parents even if they meet the legal requirements. One of the first stories we heard about bachelor adoption was from an orphanage director who turned down a man's application to adopt a child from the orphanage even though they had foundlings available for adoption at the time. Although qualified by the law, it was likely that bachelors, long stigmatized as "bare branches," would be at the end of the list of eligible adopters for many orphanages, making adoption outside of government channels a necessity even if they met the legal requirements.

In the 1990s, relatively high levels of abandonment made it possible for at least some bachelors who wanted to become fathers to adopt foundlings outside of state orphanages. This became more difficult as abandonment declined in the 2000s, just at a time the skewed sex ratios created in this era also began to affect the marriage market for men of marriageable age. But in the 1990s and early 2000s we found a number of bachelors who adopted and raised foundling daughters. Like other de facto adoptions, their cases highlight the problem of hukou for adopted children, especially foundlings.

Sun Bingfa,[13] who we met in 2009 at fifty-nine years old, did not set out to adopt a child. In the late 1990s when there were many foundlings in this area, he was approached about adopting an abandoned baby that was found by a relative in the wake of flooding in the area. At that time he declined, feeling he did not have the conditions to raise a child. Perhaps he thought there was still a chance he might get married. But in the winter of 2001 on his way home from a work site about two hours away, he heard a baby crying on the roadside and found a newborn wrapped in a small dirty blanket. There was no note and no one around. He could not leave the child there, so he picked her up and brought her home; he soon decided to keep and raise her. It seemed to him that this baby was somehow fated to be his adopted daughter. When we met them, Qianqian was eight, and they were living with Bingfa's younger brother Bingyi, age fifty, also a bachelor. Qianqian referred to both as father, Big Father (Da Ba) and Third Father (San Ba) because Bingyi was the third of three brothers. Though their home was extremely poor and a bit ramshackle, the area where Qianqian studied and slept, and where the family ate meals, was well kept and contained almost all of the family's possessions, including a large carefully folded pile of color-ful clothes for Qianqian (mostly hand-me-downs from neighbors and relatives), children's schoolbooks, a desk, a few toys, and a TV. When we arrived unexpectedly one night, the three of them were sitting together in this room at a small foldaway table eating dinner that San Ba had made—a vegetable dish, a chicken dish, and a bowl of noodles.

This three-person family lived across the street from members of their extended family, who occasionally stopped by and helped them out. Bingfa was himself the son of an adopted son who had been orphaned in a flood in the 1930s, becoming one of three sons of the Sun patriarch. Bingfa's father in turn had had three sons and two daughters. Only one of the sons, the second, was able to marry and produce children, perhaps reflecting the lowly status and rela-tive poverty of the family branch descended from an adopted son. Bingyi, the third son, had been married briefly to a "Sichuan bride," for whom he said he had paid a "bride price" (*lijin*), but she ran away after less than two months. He heard that she quickly remarried and then left this husband within a year. He laughed as he told the story, but it was no doubt a painful, humiliating episode, emblematic of the low and powerless status of a poor bachelor in rural China, leaving him alone and even poorer. In contrast to the dominant image of men like Bingyi—poor "bare branches" prone to illegal and violent behavior—Bingyi appeared more as a powerless victim of a scam that took advantage of his low status on the margins of "decent" society. Also in contrast to the common characterization of men like Bingfa and Bingyi as prone to socially irresponsible behavior such as gambling, drinking, and petty violence,[14] these men tried hard to maintain a clean and orderly home for their daughter despite their evident poverty, using their meager earnings to provide her with a good diet, books and school supplies, and a few extra treats such as a toy watch and the sausage snacks that Qianqian was fond of. Living on the outskirts of the encroaching city, Bingfa and Bingyi had only a tiny plot of land and neither had ever had a real trade. Both were illiterate and unskilled. Bingfa worked as a day laborer at construction sites. Bingyi, who appeared more frail, tried his hand at carpentry but was not good at it. More recently, he set up a small barbershop in the front of their house, taking advantage of their home's location on the side of a busy road leading into the city. Business was not very good.

When we first met them, Qianqian still had no hukou after eight years. Shortly after he found her, Bingfa went to many offices to try to arrange a hukou. He said that because he was too poor to afford bribes, he got nowhere. Periodically, he would try again. When Qianqian was about five, a local official, a friend of a relative, suggested that he put her in the local orphanage for a brief period and then adopt her back, allowing the government orphanage to process her papers and give her a legal hukou. Qianqian overheard this conversation and ran away and hid; many hours later Bingfa found her hiding upstairs in a storage area crying behind a locked door. She was terrified of being sent to the orphanage and would not unlock the door until Bingfa promised not to follow the official's advice. Better not to have a hukou than to put her through this, forcing her to live in an orphanage for even one day, he said. In early 2010, a politically connected cousin finally was able to obtain a local hukou for Qianqian, at last making her a legal citizen of the small city she lived in. Her primary schoolteachers had accepted her without a hukou, but going to middle school would be impossible unless she had a hukou. Qianqian was a good student and hoped to continue through high school.

When we learned the details of Qianqian's hukou, we glimpsed further into the subterfuge that birth planning regulations might set in motion and the resultant masquerades that could be found in household registers. When Qianqian finally got a hukou, it was as an overquota daughter of her uncle, Sun Bingya, her adoptive father's second brother, not her adoptive father. Qianqian could not be put on the household registry of Bingfa as an adopted daughter because he already had a "daughter" in his hukou book. The "daughter" in Bingfa's registry was actually his second brother Bingya's first child, who was put on his registry seventeen years earlier so that Bingya and his wife could quickly have another child under the same birth permission certificate in an effort to have a son. When Bingya's wife was pregnant with a second child, she ran away to avoid being forced to abort, just as a ferocious birth planning campaign moved into the area. If she were caught, she would have to abort her late-term pregnancy. With no time to spare, local officials put her mother-in-law, Bingya and Bingfa's mother, in jail to try to force the pregnant woman to return for the abortion. After about a week, Bingfa convinced the officials to let him take his elderly mother's place, so he spent a few weeks in jail. By then the son was born.

In order to save the officials' political record, a deal was struck to register the barely year-old daughter in the household of Bingfa, who was childless, and the newborn son could then be registered as the firstborn of Bingfa's brother and sister-in-law without the officials registering any overquota children. This arrangement had stayed on the books for seventeen years, which was probably one of the reasons Bingfa could not register Qianqian's adoption since only childless people were allowed to adopt unless the child was living in an orphanage at the time of adoption. Now in 2011, using political connections and paying a fine, Qianqian would be registered as the overquota daughter of Bingfa's second brother, while Bingfa's second brother's actual daughter remained registered as Bingfa's adopted daughter. As the adults in the room had an animated conversation about these past events, arrests, and the manipulations of records and children, Qianqian sat on a small stool and listened intently. I asked her quietly if she understood what was being said and she nodded, "Yes, a little bit," with a concerned look on her face. I said, "You live with your Baba and have a hukou now. That is all that matters." She smiled and agreed. As we were talking, the now seventeen-year-old boy for whom all of this was done walked through the room; I realized he was both the older brother and the cousin of Qianqian.

These very complicated family relationships were products of the ways people coped with the birth planning regime of this era. We found many other equally complicated examples, some much more difficult than this one in which the girl's actual status as a de facto adoptee of Sun Bingfa was known to all. This story also illustrates how an adopted child was folded into an extended family and even became one of the threads that knit them together as they circulated their children through and around the regulations of the birth planning regime of the late twentieth and early twenty-first centuries. Above all, perhaps, it demonstrates how a foundling daughter could create a family for two bachelor members of this complicated extended kin group.

Rural Migrants and Adoption in the 2000s

As migration increased through the 1990s and first decade of the twenty-first century, many people in inland agricultural areas went to look for work in the southern and eastern coastal regions where there were more nonagricultural jobs for migrant workers. In 2003 Dai Biao[15] and his spouse Wu Lianfang left their village in central China and went to Guangzhou with their two boys, then eight and six years old. Dai had a job as a driver for a company, and Wu found a job as a daytime nanny. They told us there were many foundlings (*qiying*) in Guangzhou in 2003 compared to their home area in central China, perhaps because of the large migrant population and because of birth planning crackdowns reported in nearby rural areas. Shortly after they arrived they heard about a baby girl found in a nearby park, but, though tempted, they passed up the opportunity to adopt her because they were not settled. Like many others from their area, they had hoped for a girl when they gave birth to their second son in violation of birth planning regulations in their village, thinking a girl and a boy would be ideal. They had just finished paying off the birth planning fine for their second son a few months before they left for Guangzhou. Now they were far from the control of birth planning authorities in their village. Thus, after working in Guangzhou for several months, when Dai and Wu found an abandoned baby girl early one morning, bundled in a blanket by their neighbor's doorstep, they decided on the spot that they wanted to keep her. When they picked up the tiny baby, they saw she had a piece of her umbilical cord still attached to her belly, indicating that she was a newborn. When they called home with the news, friends and relatives offered mixed opinions about their decision, some saying "she is not your birth child, you should not keep her, it will cost you a lot of money to have a baby in Guangzhou," while others supported the idea of keeping her because they had no daughter.

"She is a newborn and will be the same as your own birth child," one relative said to them, echoing their own feelings. But keeping her was indeed expensive and stressful. Baby formula in Guangzhou was expensive, and their new daughter was a sickly baby, with chronic diarrhea. They had to take her to the hospital many times in the first few months, costing them more than 10,000 yuan. Yet they never doubted their choice, they said.

Worse family health problems soon befell them. Before they left Guangzhou to return home at the New Year's, Wu discovered that she was HIV positive, which in turn led to the discovery that Dai and both their sons also were infected with HIV/AIDS. Wu sold blood in one of the central rural China collection stations in the mid-1990s and, like many others in her area, contracted HIV due to the unhygienic collection methods. She had apparently transmitted the virus to her husband and to both sons at birth. Now the only healthy member of their family was their infant daughter. Shortly after discovering their health status they returned home, and the parents soon joined the national free antiretroviral (ARV) drug program that had just been established in their village, an area close to the epicenter of the rural China HIV/AIDS epidemic. However, there were no pediatric drugs available at the time. Tragically, their younger son soon became very ill and did not respond to late efforts to use the available adult ARV medications. He died the next year, just before pediatric drugs became available in their area. Fortunately, their older son did better on the adult medications and became stable after joining the national ARV program, as did his parents.

Upon returning home, Dai and Wu registered their daughter with local authorities as a birth child so they could obtain a hukou for her. The village leader knew she was a "found" child but agreed to register her as an overquota birth that they allegedly had while working outside the area. Indeed, this was the only way to get her a hukou. Wu and Dai were not qualified to adopt because they were

not childless, and it would be difficult to get a hukou for a foundling that came from outside the area. Furthermore, because two of
their children had AIDS, there would be no fine for this alleged
overquota birth. It was the practice in this area not to fine AIDS-
affected families for birth planning violations and to stop the collection of fines for past offenses, as some families in this area took
many years to pay off their birth planning fines. The cruel irony was
that Dai and Wu had only recently paid off the fine for their second
son who was now dead. Life was harsh and unfair.

After the death of their younger son, Dai and Wu decided that
when their own health was stabilized on ARV treatment, they
would have another child. Even though their other son was doing
fairly well on ARV treatment, they were frantically worried that
he would also die, leaving only one healthy child, the only healthy
person in the family. They learned that with the help of maternal
ARV treatment before birth and for the baby just after birth, there
was a high likelihood that they could give birth to a healthy child.
They said that when they learned this, they did not care if they had
a boy or girl as long as it was healthy so they did not try to find out
the sex of the fetus. When their adopted daughter was five, they
gave birth to a healthy baby girl. When asked if they now had any
regrets about adopting their oldest daughter, they said absolutely
not; the happiest thing in their lives now was having two healthy
children. They both brought joy to the family and would always
have each other even if the other family members did not survive.
We knew of at least two other mothers with HIV/AIDS in this area
who had healthy babies with the help of close monitoring and pre-
and postnatal treatment with ARV medication. With a local policy that exempted AIDS-affected families from birth quotas, and a
national policy to supply free ARV drugs to HIV/AIDS patients,
including pre- and postnatal treatment for pregnant women and
their newborns, local officials in this area behaved with tolerance

and compassion for the reproductive choices these families made, including those involving adoption.

We talked to Dai at length about the issue of adoption in his family. He was adamant that his daughter should never know she was a "found" child. Her hukou was that of a birth child, and she was treated in every way as if she were born to them. He said he even forgets that she is not their birth child. We asked him why this secret was so important; surely keeping the secret was a burden for them since some people already know the truth. He looked at us and asked, "Why would I tell her we found her abandoned in the street? Why would I make her feel she is different than her sister? She is not different in our minds; she has been with us since the first hour of her life." What if a relative or the village official lets the truth slip? "She will never believe them," he replied confidently. "Even her hukou says she is our birth child." Telling her she was a foundling would create an unnecessary emotional burden for the child; they would spare her these feelings.

Another couple with AIDS from this same area of rural central China also adopted an abandoned infant that they found while working in Suzhou, another area with many migrants. The infant was a healthy newborn boy found next to a public bathroom; they guessed he might have been born to a young unmarried migrant worker who gave birth in secret, left the child on the spot, and ran away. Any birth to an unwed mother, in addition to the social stigma, is considered "out of plan," subject to a heavy fine and then counted against any births the mother might be permitted in a future marriage. She would also lose her job if employed by a factory. To the migrant couple that found the baby, it was an unbelievable gift. They had just learned that they and their six-year-old daughter were all HIV positive, so finding this healthy infant son was a blessing. Their family now had a future, and they planned to stay healthy long enough to help their son build that future. They had already found the land upon which they would build his house when he married, and they talked about it often. While their daughter was doing well on ARV drugs, they assumed that she could never marry, have children, or live a normal life. Like them, she was condemned forever by this fearsome disease contracted by her parents through blood selling and unknowingly passed on to her at birth. When we first met this couple, they did not know that it was possible for them to have a healthy baby with the help of ARV medication, so it seemed that the foundling son bore the heavy weight of the family's future by himself. However, when they learned of others' success, they decided that they too wanted to try to have a healthy sibling for their son and the next year gave birth to a healthy girl.

In the meantime, at the suggestion of local officials, they, like Dai and Wu, registered the boy as their birth child and immediately got a proper hukou for him. Although the adoption of a foundling after having a child was a violation of the adoption law, they were permitted by birth planning to have a second birth six years after the birth of a girl; furthermore, as an AIDS-affected family, they would also be exempt from fines. Thus the ruse, suggested by a local official to save everyone "trouble," was a perfect solution to get the foundling boy a legal status in their family.

Hidden Children: Fostering, Paper Adoptions, and the Problem of Hukou

Although many birth parents made the decision to secretly relinquish a child in order to hide the birth from authorities, most parents who wanted to hide out-of-plan children sought and found ways of concealing their birth without permanently relinquishing their children.[16] A common pattern for hiding children without relinquishing them was through temporary adoptions or foster care arrangements, arranged wholly as a means of hiding a child and disguising its true identity for a limited period of time. One frequent strategy was to hide the pregnancy and then send the child away to friends or relatives in other villages. Maternal relatives, who were usually located in other villages, often provided this kind of temporary refuge. Hiding a child in another village might involve finding someone who was legally qualified to "adopt" the child on paper, such as a childless bachelor or widow who could put the child on their household register. Or a child might remain unregistered in another village, posing as a visiting niece or nephew until returning to their birth families after several years, such as after the birth of a son or when it was time to go to school. Sometimes the child would stay with birth parents under a false identity. We saw a variation of all of these strategies in the story above, whereby Sun Bingya put his daughter on the household register of his brother Sun Bingfa, a childless bachelor. In this case local officials were complicit, so the arrangement remained within the birth parent's village, with the child being raised at home by her parents under a legal identity as their adopted niece.

THE DOCTORS' SECOND SON

These kinds of arrangements could become very complicated and involve elaborate masquerades. In the late 1990s we met a family of two doctors working at a hospital in a large county town[17] who had two sons, ages ten and five. The second pregnancy was hidden, and the child's existence as their son was a secret to everyone but a few close relatives and friends. The cost to the parents if the illegal birth was discovered would be enormous—not only a huge fine many times their yearly income, but the loss of both jobs, forcing them to find work outside the area as migrants. Although the family of four lived together in town, the youngest boy was registered as the "adopted foundling son" of his mother's older sister, a widow who lived in the countryside. Although the widow already had an older son, which should have prohibited an adoption under the law and birth planning regulations, due to local sympathy for her sad situation living alone as a recent widow, village officials allowed her to register the "found" child as her son after she paid a fine for an overquota adoption.

Although the "adoption" was entirely a ruse, in public the five-year-old boy, like the rest of the family, had to maintain the fiction by calling his aunt his "mother," his mother his "aunt," and his father his "uncle." Ostensibly he lived in town with his "aunt" and "uncle," where he attended a private kindergarten, because his "mother" was single and poor and the village schooling inferior to what his prosperous "relatives" could provide. The child also had to be careful in school not to tip off the teachers that his "older cousin," who often came to pick him up, was really his older brother. Fortunately, in local kinship terms a child could call an older cousin *gege*, the same term for older brother. But the parents lived in constant fear that the young boy would slip. One night when we were having dinner in a restaurant with the family, including the aunt, a local official stopped by our table to chat for a few minutes. When he left, I noticed that both boys were gone; they had sneaked out so that the younger boy wouldn't make a mistake in front of the official. The older brother was responsible for protecting his younger brother in these kinds of public situations, so he quickly got him out of the restaurant. The parents said it was a heavy burden for the ten-year-old. The mother said she lived in a constant state of anxiety and sometimes wanted to come forward to tell the truth and get it over with, but the consequences loomed as too large.

We found many more hidden and unregistered boys than we expected, believing, as the scant research on this topic suggests, that the vast majority of "black children" are girls. Boys constituted nearly 45 percent of our nonrandom sample of hidden and unregistered children, although the percentage of boys declined in the

1990s. Most of these boys were overquota, born to parents who had already filled their allowed births with one or more daughters; occasionally, like the case above, they were second or even third sons. One village couple in pursuit of a daughter after a firstborn son gave birth to three overquota boys, running away each time to hide the unauthorized pregnancy and the birth. The three overquota hidden boys were all given girl's names and chided throughout their childhood that they had bankrupted their parents in an unsuccessful pursuit of a daughter; hence they owed their parents a granddaughter. The three younger boys were high academic achievers, each hoping to repay their poor parents for the huge fines they eventually had to pay to obtain hukous so they could go to middle school and college.

HIDING AT GRANDMA'S HOUSE

A common pattern involving girls was hiding the birth of a second or third girl in order to preserve another chance to have a boy. In one typical case,[18] a second-born daughter was sent to her maternal grandmother's village in another area, where her grandmother was able to arrange an "adoption" with an older bachelor in the village. The child was registered and received a hukou in the man's family as his adopted daughter, but she lived with her grandmother. She spent eight years with her grandmother, at which time a younger brother was finally born, making it possible for her to return to her parent's home. In the meantime a third daughter had been born and adopted out via a "targeted abandonment" on the doorstep of a childless couple in another village. When the second daughter returned home, her parents paid local officials to transfer her hukou to their village. After she returned, local birth planning officials soon identified the boy as a third birth, fined the family a years' income, and required that the mother be sterilized. However, the goal of having a son had been accomplished.

We never got a chance to talk separately with the temporarily hidden second daughter about how she felt about being sent away so her parents could have a boy. That she had some feelings about this was suggested when she sharply contradicted her father's account of what happened. Asked how old his second daughter was when she returned home, the father could not remember exactly, but he said she was "only gone a few years," implying she returned at a young age. The daughter, then fifteen, interjected from the other side of the room, "It was not a few years. I came back when I was eight." She also corrected her father on the issue of her hukou. He said he had arranged to have the hukou from the fake adoption transferred to their home when she moved back; however, the girl pointedly added that she was still "not listed as a daughter in this family" on the hukou but had a separate hukou for this village. This teenager was far from oblivious about what had happened to her, paying attention even to the details of her still-irregular hukou status. What did she think about the third daughter, the *meimei* she never met, who was permanently sent out of the family for the sake of her younger brother? We never had a chance to ask her; it wasn't even clear how much she knew about the third *meimei*. Her father told us later that he kept an eye on the third daughter from afar but said the girl did not know who he was and said the adoptive parents would not be happy if he ever identified himself or spoke to her. If the second daughter was resentful about what had happened to her, at least she had been brought back to her own family. Furthermore, a few years after she came home, a baby cousin, a prohibited out-of-plan daughter born to one of her uncles after he had a son, was taken away by officials in an event that traumatized her uncle's family and left her aunt in a state of mental collapse.[19] This teen was quite aware of the vulnerability of being an out-of-plan girl and knew that "hiding" did not always work out.

Although each case was different in details, this general pattern was remarkably common in this area in the 1990s and early 2000s. In the 1990s, the coordination among villages was often loose, especially in the periods between birth planning campaigns, and local officials did not really care about the birth planning "problems" of other areas. Because of the persistence of patrilocal residence patterns in villages, maternal relatives often played an important role in hiding children because they usually lived in other villages, under the jurisdiction of other officials.[20]

"TWINNING"

Temporarily hiding a daughter with maternal relatives or friends was one of the most common masquerades we learned about. But the variations were as diverse as people's imaginations. After several years of visiting an area, I learned that young teen "twins," a boy and a girl widely known to me and their friends as "The Twins," were in fact born eleven months apart, sharing one birth permission certificate, and registered as twins. The boy was born first, so the fake "twinning" was the only way to get in a second birth without being fined. As we have seen there were many adopted children who were claimed as birth children, as well as birth children who were claimed as "found" adopted children or as visiting nieces or nephews from another area. With noncompliance reported to be as high as 30 percent in some areas in the mid-1990s, one would expect hiding strategies to be diverse and widespread as well.[21]

The Costs of Being a Hidden Child

Most hidden children, especially those who were circulated among friends and relatives by their birth parents, eventually obtained a hukou in some way, allowing them to leave the category of "black child." Some did so by assuming a false identity with a hukou that obscured their true identity, others remained unregistered longer, perhaps in their parent's own home, until their parents found a way to register them, sometimes taking advantage of periodic amnesties when fines were lowered in an effort to get "black children" registered. This happened around every ten-year census and sometimes in between when sample surveys may be conducted. By middle school age most had a hukou of some type although some did not.

The material consequences of having a "black" status, as reported by parents, included missed childhood inoculations, an inability to register for school other than rural primary schools (although some schools would accept extra money to allow the child to go to school without records), a loss of medical or social welfare benefits that might be attached to a parent's work unit or to a local county, town, or village hukou. An older teen without a hukou could not go to junior middle school, high school, or college, could not get any kind of state job, or other work in the public sector, and could not even register to marry. Without a hukou there was no entitlement to family land rights. Even recruitment to a nonstate factory usually required an identity card. Unskilled migrant work was likely the only path for a livelihood for a person who could not gain a hukou during their childhood.

Parents also reported less tangible but real psychological consequences associated with being a "black child" for even a short period of time, noting a "black child personality" or mentality characterized as introverted, withdrawn, lacking self-confidence, feeling excluded from the family, and looked down upon by self and others. This seemed to apply to "sent away" children as well, even if they had a hukou under a false identity. Parents reported this very early in a child's development as some children sensed their inferiority to others at a young age, becoming aware of their lower status, their lack of an official existence, or the lack of a right to exist at all. Even young children might remark, "I should never have been born." One father of a six-year-old adopted girl told us that his daughter cried because she could not go to the "good" school with her friends as she had no hukou. Instead, she would be sent to a nearby village school where she could attend primary school for an extra fee. What was wrong with her, she asked. "Why am I this kind of child?" Her father, who had tried but not yet succeeded in getting her a hukou in the wake of a local registration effort, was both sad and angry to see her suffer these feelings of inferiority at such a young age.

Hiding strategies that kept children in the birth family might avoid worse losses for both child and parents than those entailed in abandonment or permanently sending a child away to be adopted; in some ways these strategies seemed merely to mimic traditional childcare practices among extended families. But they often exacted emotional as well as concrete costs for the child and parents.

One university graduate,[22] who lived most of her childhood with her grandparents and gained an official hukou when she was around twelve, said that as a child she always knew "I should never have been born, I should not have existed." Unlike her siblings who stayed at home, she never felt worthy of her parents' love or resources. Obtaining her hukou was a great financial burden for the family, because they finally had to pay a huge fine as well as pay several bribes for the hukou. Even as a young adult, she still felt guilty for the poverty she caused. In the end she said her need to prove her right to exist drove her to study obsessively, harder than anyone else in her family or school, leading to high scores and entrance into a first-tier university, an ironic and hard-earned benefit of her childhood status as a "black child."

Another college student[23] recounted how she was sent away at one year of age to live with her maternal grandmother for eight years while her younger sister, who was born using the same birth permit, stayed home. She was finally allowed to rejoin her family when a younger brother was born. Until she went to college, her hukou was under the name of an elderly bachelor in her grandmother's village, ostensibly her adoptive father, a man she never lived with but on whose doorstep she was allegedly found. Now that she has transferred her hukou to the city where she attended university and graduate school, she says she no longer cares about her past status. Although she is very close to her parents and two siblings, and has great sympathy for her hardworking, illiterate mother, she cried as she recounted this story, surprising even herself. She said she just buried how she felt most of her childhood and has tried not to blame her parents or resent her siblings. Instead, she expressed bitter hatred for her paternal grandmother who had pressured her parents to hide her as soon as her sister was born so that they could eventually have a son.[24]

Sometimes sending a child away to hide her created rifts that were so severe they could not be mended. A second daughter sent away by parents to live with a relative in a neighboring province returned after the birth of a son, around the time she was old enough to go to primary school.[25] When she returned to her family, she was immediately homesick for the home where she was raised. She did not get along with her siblings and rarely talked to her parents. She spoke with a heavy accent from the dialect of the area she was raised, almost unintelligible to local children, and this affected her in school and in the neighborhood, where she was marked as an outsider by the other children. Her parents said her personality had been deeply affected by her "black" status, turning her into an introverted and sometimes angry child who resented her parents for bringing her back and missed her foster family. The parents were regretful and felt that they had permanently damaged their daughter by hiding her and sending her away. They said they loved her but that she did not love them. They recommended to others that, whatever the cost, they should keep their own children at home. We heard this same sentiment from several parents who had temporarily hidden children.

While most parents found a way to bring their child out of the shadows by the time they were supposed to go to school, either through amnesties or by obtaining a hukou by other means, at least some unregistered children remained in the category of "black child," a noncitizen in their country of birth, for an extended period. This is a problem that continues until today, despite sporadic efforts at reform.[26] Obtaining hukou for out-of-plan children was more difficult in cities and township and county-level towns where a one-child policy often prevails and where hukou rights are controlled more strictly than in villages, in part because they bring greater entitlements. Not surprisingly, we also found in our research on unregistered children that a disproportionate number of "black children" were adopted children. About one-third of the children in our sample of unregistered children were adopted, a much higher percentage than in the general population. Furthermore, in sharp contrast to the pool of healthy young children found in orphanages in the 1990s and early 2000s, over 95 percent of whom were girls, nearly 30 percent of these hidden adopted children were healthy boys, with the percentage declining somewhat throughout the 1990s. Adopted boys were relinquished through abandonment and through surreptitiously arranged adoptions like the more numerous adopted girls, although girls were more likely to have been found abandoned by their adoptive parents.[27] Adopted children, regardless of gender, were likely to remain unregistered longer than others because of the restrictions on adoption and consequent restrictions on obtaining a hukou for adopted children. Because girls were more heavily represented among adopted children, they were at higher risk of remaining unregistered throughout their childhood. Policies and local regulations in many areas explicitly withheld hukou from de facto adopted children even when parents were willing to pay fines.[28] As we will see, in 2011 the Ministry of Civil Affairs made this a national policy. In other areas that offered a path to legalize a child's status, few if any parents of adopted foundlings could hope to produce or fabricate the necessary documents for legal registration.[29] Regardless of regulations, local officials were reluctant to register adopted foundlings, not wanting to add an "overquota" child to their jurisdiction. The inability to obtain a legal status often amounted to a double or even triple stigma in a child's life—that of being a "black child" and an adopted child, one who often started life as a "discarded" out-of-plan child.

The longer time it takes adopted children to gain a hukou not only creates emotional liabilities but also interferes with their childhood health care and their schooling far into their childhood. A study in 2004 confirmed that although adopted children were likely to do as well as birth children in terms of basic physical well-being and family care, they were disadvantaged by lower rates of childhood immunization and school enrollment, both likely to be a consequence of lacking a hukou.[30] Finding a second family, even one willing to pay high fines and fees for their adopted child, did not automatically overcome the numerous legal obstacles to citizenship and erase the liabilities of being a relinquished out-of-plan child in this era. Some adopted children struggled for years to become citizens, years during which they lacked basic entitlements and basic protections and rights, including even the right to a family. As we will see below, more than a few adopted children lost their second family because their adoptive parents could not find a way to legalize their child's status in order to send them to school or otherwise bring them out of the shadows. Some of these children ended up in the pool of orphanage children made available for international adoption.

The central government and Civil Affairs ministry have periodically called for amnesties and registration drives. Some cities, such as Beijing, have passed policies that require that children be granted hukou in their place of residence by local authorities. While these reform efforts have retrospectively helped many children establish a legal existence, the reforms have been hard to use and, since they are primarily implemented as amnesties, they never solve the problem for new entrants into the unregistered category.

In 2010 we met a frustrated adoptive father in Hefei, living in a new area of the city that had recently engulfed his village, who was trying to obtain a legal status for his three-and-a-half-year-old adopted daughter. A major stumbling block, as usual, was that he was not childless at the time of adoption; he and his wife had an eight-year-old son. Under a 2008 hukou reform effort for de facto adopted children, he was trying to gather and file all of the paperwork necessary to get a hukou for his three-year-old foundling daughter. He told us he had already spent nearly three years and 50,000 yuan in the process and still had not obtained her hukou. Among other things, he had to provide and pay for a DNA test to prove the girl was not biologically related to him or his wife. Furthermore, he had to provide neighborhood testimony, verified by police interviews, that he had in fact found this child abandoned outside his door in 2007. When we spoke to him, he was upset because his daughter could not even attend kindergarten in this recently incorporated urban area until he obtained her hukou. "Is she not entitled to a hukou and an education like every other child?" he asked exasperated by his ordeal.[31]

The problem of hukou for out-of-plan children has never been solved, especially for adopted children. New hidden children are created every year, even if their numbers have declined as fertility declines and even if periodic reforms, as amnesties, eliminate some "black children" from previous years. Birth planning regulations continue to deny hukou to out-of-plan children as a matter of stated policy, as does the recent adoption regulation proposed by the Ministry of Civil Affairs and its Center for Children's Welfare and Adoption in 2011. Laws penalizing out-of-plan births and adoptions maintain a stranglehold on registration requirements that undercut hukou reform for children, making the reforms extremely difficult if not impossible to use. Regardless of various reform efforts over the years, birth planning and adoption policies have invariably punished and disadvantaged the product of prohibited reproduction, the out-of-plan child, as well as the people who produce and care for them. None of the recent reforms, including birth planning reforms that increase the exceptions to the one-child rule, have eliminated this problem, the fundamental abrogation of out-of-plan children's basic right to a legal existence and citizenship in their country of birth.

From "Unwanted Abandoned Girls" to "Stolen Children": The Circulation of Out-of-Plan Children in the 2000s

In the mid-1990s the rise of international adoption from China was accompanied by media images of large numbers of unwanted Chinese girls languishing and dying in overcrowded orphanages, as portrayed by the British documentary *The Dying Rooms* (1995). Ten years later, new media scandals emerged of orphanages having to "buy babies" to "sell" into international adoption. Stories of baby traffickers colluding with orphanage officials in the central province of Hunan hit the news in a high-profile government trial in 2006,[1] followed a few years later with stories of children "stolen" by officials to sell to orphanages in Guizhou and similar stories emerging again in Shaoyang, Hunan.[2] All of this was joined by frequent media accounts of kidnapping by criminal gangs, captured in a 2008 documentary *China's Stolen Children*,[3] filmed by the same people as *The Dying Rooms*. In the last five years, almost weekly reports appear in the Chinese media about police crackdowns on child traffickers and their "buyers." The issue is a complicated one that finds government actors on both sides of the media stories, which sometimes obscure as much as they reveal.

The shift from a glut to a shortage of healthy "unwanted" children in state hands was revealed by the 2006 government trial of

Hunan orphanage directors for "buying" children that some orphanages in central south China, once with a seemingly limitless
supply of healthy abandoned infants, began in the early 2000s to
make efforts to draw in more children from other areas further
south because there were fewer healthy abandoned children found
in their own areas and the demand for adoption, both international
and domestic, was increasing. Orphanages that did not make these
efforts had fewer and fewer healthy children entering their gates.[4]

Not only was international adoption still growing at this time, as
international adopters and their agencies utilized the institutional
channels set up in the 1990s to facilitate its development, but also
the legal restrictions placed on domestic adopters were eased somewhat by revisions to the adoption law that took effect in 1999, lowering the legal adoption age from thirty-five to thirty and allowing
a family with a child to adopt a child "currently living in an orphanage" under certain circumstances. Furthermore, some areas established formal legal channels for childless people over thirty to adopt
a police-certified "abandoned" child "directly from society" if (and
only if) they carefully followed proper procedures to register the
child with Civil Affairs. These legal changes enlarged the number
of domestic adopters legally qualified to adopt from government
orphanages and outside of them. Thus in the early 2000s, legal domestic adoption added to the increasing international demand for
a diminishing number of healthy babies that fell into the hands of
orphanages, creating direct competition between international and
domestic adopters for the young healthy children living in orphanages and also between the orphanages and childless domestic adopters who found babies outside the orphanage.[5] As we learned in the
area of our research, de facto adoption had always greatly reduced
the number of healthy babies that came into orphanages, but now
more of them could even do so legally. As early as 2001, the director
of a medium-size orphanage fretted that his "supply" of desirable

children for international adoption would soon dry up in the face of diminishing numbers and domestic competition just as international adopters were flocking to China to adopt healthy infants.[6] In some orphanages, such as the one run by the aforementioned director, relatively wealthy international adopters were clearly favored in the early 2000s because they still usually paid higher fees ($3,000–$5,000) than could be obtained from domestic adopters (a gap that eventually disappears),[7] most of which could be kept by the orphanage, adding to the perception, echoed in the media both inside and outside China, that government orphanages were trafficking children for their own profit.[8] However, by the end of the decade the shortage of healthy young children in orphanages eventually led to waiting times of over seven years for international adopters, while most domestic adopters, even those legally qualified to adopt from a state orphanage, had no choice but to turn elsewhere to find a healthy child to adopt.[9] Reflecting the change in the population of the orphanages, international adoption finally began a rapid decline after peaking at around fourteen thousand in 2005, and the emergence of organized transregional networks facilitating de facto domestic adoption outside of government channels became apparent. These transregional networks, running from poorer areas with higher fertility to better-off areas, were quickly identified by the government as "child trafficking."

Thus in little more than a decade the ground had shifted from an abundance of "unwanted" healthy baby girls flowing into government institutions in central south China, an area that had pioneered international adoption in the 1990s, to a dearth of healthy babies available for any kind of adoption both inside and outside the orphanages.

This dynamic of lessening supply and rising demand created financial incentives that seemed to explain the baby buying and baby confiscation scandals that periodically surfaced in the media both inside and outside of China. Yet most of the stories about stealing and buying and selling children into adoption missed important underlying dynamics rooted in the population control and adoption policies and laws. As we will see, it was often less the pecuniary incentives of the market than the perverse local behavior created by the operation of birth planning pressures with its own powerful political and financial incentives on behalf of state policies that has best explained how and why children were separated from their families in many of these cases. Despite low fertility, monitoring of reproduction in the rural areas we investigated remained tight during this period, diverging from trends of lessening overt control seen in urban areas where fertility was at ultra-low levels. In rural areas that fell under strict surveillance to eliminate out-of-plan births and "illegal adoptions," reports surfaced of local officials directly pressuring parents to remove unregistered children, something we also found in interviews.

As we will see, an important thread of continuity throughout the two decades, from abandonment to confiscation, from a glut to a scourge of kidnapping, was the particular vulnerability of the unregistered "out-of-plan" child who was the object of waves of abandonment, as well as de facto adoptions, in the 1990s and the trafficking scandals in the 2000s, a category of child created not by poverty but by birth planning policies. In addition, policies suppressing customary adoption practices loomed large in creating both the increase in the number of healthy children seen in the orphanages in the 1990s and the "baby trafficking" scandals that followed in the 2000s.

Low Fertility, Skewed Sex Ratios, and the Persistence of a Two-Gender Ideal

In the area of rural central China that we studied, we could see the larger demographic changes that lay beneath the changing patterns of child circulation and tightening of the supply of adoptable children: fertility desires continued their decline from the 1990s,[10] infant relinquishment declined, and signs of unmet local demand for children emerged in our interviews as well as in media stories of children being brought in from poorer south and southwestern areas for adoptive families in central and eastern China.[11]

Anecdotally, our interviews reflected the changing fertility attitudes in the countryside. Although a two-gender family remained an often-articulated ideal, the desire to have no more than two children and the acceptability of one child, including one daughter,[12] seemed to strengthen. Unlike in the 1980s and 1990s, people were less likely to pursue multiple births in order to achieve a two-gender ideal, whether the missing gender was a boy or a girl. With the further consolidation of a small family ideal, more families with two daughters might forgo a third attempt for a son because they did not want a larger family and were unwilling to relinquish or permanently send away a daughter. Effective pressures to be sterilized after two births in this area, pressures that were particularly strong after two daughters, also limited the further pursuit of a third child.

Furthermore in this 1.5-child policy area, those with a firstborn daughter who were determined to have a son within their legal quota and within the two-child, two-gender ideal could surreptitiously subject a permitted second pregnancy to ultrasound for the purpose of prenatal sex selection.[13] With the use of this technology, the long-standing family ideal of a boy and a girl could thereby be achieved by those whose firstborn was a girl. In fact, as mentioned earlier, the 1.5-child policy areas reported the most skewed sex ratios in the country as a result of sex selecting the relatively high numbers of second births for a son, resulting in extraordinarily skewed reported sex ratios for second births while maintaining closer to normal sex ratios for first births.[14] Although this practice is usually seen as indicating stronger traditional "son preference" in these rural areas, this pattern may also be seen as a reflection of the way the 1.5-child policy interacts with the "one son and one daughter" ideals that are so prevalent in these areas, a factor that only rarely receives consideration in discussions of skewed sex ratios. Enforced stopping rules that prohibit births after a firstborn son but not after a daughter may also contribute to this skew in 1.5-child policy areas by allowing the pursuit of a son after the birth of a daughter while making the pursuit of a daughter after a son much more difficult and costly. Thus skewed sex ratios in this area do not necessarily reflect stronger son preference among the population of these rural areas than other areas.[15] Birth planning rules and a two-gender ideal among a large segment of the people can also help to explain the pattern. A couple of women explained their view that the 1.5-child policy in their area discriminated against girls precisely because it prevented mothers with a son from trying to have a daughter while it allowed mothers with a girl to try to have a boy.[16] That is why there were more boys, they said. The women's criticism of the 1.5-child policy was quite different from the more common critique in the literature that the 1.5-child policy reinforces the inferiority of girls by officially inscribing the idea that boys are more valuable than girls.[17] Implicit in the women's remarks was an assumption that people would sex select a second pregnancy after a son to get a girl just as those with a firstborn daughter do now for a son. Indeed, areas where a second birth is permitted regardless of the gender of the first birth have significantly less skewed sex ratios than other areas and second births after a son have unnaturally high rates of female births,[18] confirming the presence of a two-gender ideal.

Because a two gender–two child family remained an ideal for many in this area, those with a son might even push the envelope beyond the rules to try to have a daughter through a prohibited overquota birth. We met quite a few villagers who did so in the late 1990s and 2000s, often paying a substantial fine for the second birth,[19] a fine that some remarked was "worth it" to get a daughter. Of course some people ended up with a second son instead; it was harder to subject an illegal second pregnancy to ultrasound because the pregnancy itself needed to be hidden. A couple of these mothers spontaneously remarked when casually asked about their second child, "I wanted a girl" to explain why they had an overquota birth after a firstborn son. One woman on a village street holding an adorable six-month-old infant boy said to him playfully in front of me, "You were supposed to be a girl!" It was not clear how often, if ever, people resorted to the use of ultrasound to make sure the second birth after a son would be the hoped-for daughter. After the early 2000s people did not openly discuss the use of ultrasound because of the stiff penalties associated with it, including penalties for the doctors. We talked to the close relatives of a doctor in our research area who was fined 200,000 yuan and jailed for three months in 2008 for running a clinic that performed prenatal sex identification and abortions, in addition to helping to arrange adoptions for out-of-plan babies that birth parents wanted to hide, something that the government labels as child trafficking if caught.[20] But despite the stiff penalties, it was clear that prenatal sex selective services were available surreptitiously throughout this area in the 2000s and that on occasion they were used by women with sons to insure a daughter would result from a prohibited second or third birth.[21] The desire for a daughter that we saw in adoption patterns in the 1990s and early 2000s continued to be articulated by people we talked to in these rural areas throughout the first decade of the twenty-first century even though part of this area had one of the highest reported sex ratios in the country, almost all of it concentrated in second or higher births among those who already had daughters. Such are the complexities and contradictions produced by the way policies interact with a dynamic popular culture.

As shown elsewhere, trends consolidating lower fertility desires, including the illegal use of ultrasound for second or higher order births, reduced the level of noncompliance with birth planning quotas and the overt clash with birth planning forces.[22] From all reports, it seems clear that infant abandonment of out-of-plan children, a major indication of noncompliance in the 1990s, declined significantly in this area. As a result, those who wanted to adopt, either because they were childless or because they lacked a daughter, found it much harder to do so than in the 1990s and early 2000s. As one father who adopted a daughter in the mid-1990s said to us in 2010: "It used to be that you didn't need to go any further than your front door to find a child to adopt. Now you can go out and search for months and ask everyone you know and still not find one." Abandonment, whether targeted at doorsteps or on the roads, something that had made adoption relatively easy in the 1990s, was mostly a thing of the past and along with it the ready supply of adoptable healthy infant daughters in this area. The few cases we found in 2009–11 turned out to be staged to deceive officials who had to certify a child was "abandoned" in order to make a legal adoption possible.

Although fertility desires declined and abandonment virtually disappeared in this area, birth planning surveillance, such as frequent pregnancy testing with mandatory abortions of discovered out-of-plan pregnancies and mandatory sterilization after second births, became more regularized, thorough, and indeed relentless in the countryside during the first decade of the 2000s. Our observations run counter to the view held by many scholars that after the sometimes violent rural campaigns of the early and mid-1990s, the focus of birth planning implementation began to shift away from administrative coercion toward providing client-centered health services more fitting the new attitudes and changing socioeconomic conditions emerging in China.[23] This no doubt describes birth planning trends in urban areas, where fertility has long been extremely low, far below replacement levels, and where the population increasingly was trusted to govern its own fertility. Some rural areas may also have experienced policy relaxation and reorientation during the period after the mid-1990s. However, in the rural areas we studied this was not the case in the 2000s. Although birth planning became more orderly and in this sense more "lawful" than the ferocious campaigns of the first two decades, and the population became more compliant, it would be hard to characterize it as less administratively stringent and coercive. Most people we spoke to about birth planning, including local officials, claimed that birth planning became "stricter" than ever by the middle of the first decade of the 2000s and remained so until after the end of the decade.[24] Reports of harsh implementation, including forced abortions, continue into the present.[25]

We found that heightened surveillance and pressure on local officials to eliminate out-of-plan births or face punishment, referred to as the "one vote veto rule," led to routinized monitoring of women's bodies and to intensified efforts to find unregistered out-of-plan children in order to levy high fines and sometimes remove "illegal" children from the area by confiscating them from families. At times the latter crossed the line between illegally adopted children, who had always been subject to seizure, and unregistered birth children whose origins were left "unclear," as a spate of media reports and our own research indicate. Most of these cases show that such children were usually taken from friends or relatives who were temporarily fostering and hiding them for their parents; but occasionally they were taken directly from their own parents. This latter phenomenon seemed to be a product of the birth planning regime in its third decade, when it was harder to slip through the cracks than in earlier decades when birth planning depended more on campaigns that waxed and waned and noncompliance was very widespread.

Several local officials said that birth planning was further intensified after the abolition of the agricultural tax, starting around 2004 in this area, because this freed up more time for local officials to concentrate on enforcing birth planning regulations, such as sending a local official to chase down a villager trying to escape with an out-of-plan pregnancy or avoid a mandatory sterilization after a second birth. The abolition of this tax also eliminated a source of local funding that needed to be replaced, so collecting more birth planning fines may also have helped local finances. Other areas in the country also used their resources to find and bring back people who were wanted for birth planning violations.[26] In the 1990s it was likely that leaving the area more or less assured that you were both "out of sight and out of mind," that local officials would not bother to chase you or try to coordinate with others, although you might (or might not) be fined when you returned.

Confiscation of Out-of-Plan Children since 1990

In 2011, Hunan villager Yuan Chaoren told a Caixin reporter that before 1997 birth planning officials smashed houses, fined people, and sometimes imprisoned the family head as punishment for illegal births. But, he said, "after 2000 they haven't smashed houses. They abduct children."[27]

While removing unregistered children from families appeared to reporters to be a new phenomena in the 2000s, we found that the confiscation of children or its threat by local officials accompanied earlier birth planning efforts to crack down on local adoption, which sometimes included taking adopted children from adopters who did not meet the legal requirements (or whose children did not), including proper registration. This also made it risky to hide children with friends or relatives in temporary foster arrangements from which they might be seized as illegally adopted children.[28] Local officials also sometimes became involved in helping to hide overquota children by taking them from parents who wanted to avoid fines and sterilization in a kind of arranged "abandonment" that kept the local official's record clear while hiding the overquota birth for the parents, who thereby avoided fines and sterilization but lost the child. The lines between "willingly" handing over a child, being pressured by circumstances to abandon a child, or having a child taken by force were obscured under birth planning policies that punished people for having children and made the children themselves "illegal."[29] As many cases of coerced relinquishment and government confiscation reveal, the unregistered, out-of-plan child was at highest risk of being subject to these practices in various ways. Many child trafficking cases show the same pattern.

The Vulnerability of the Adopted Foundling:
The Risk of Losing a Second Family

One of the first adoptive families that we met when we started this research in 1996 recounted how five years earlier local birth planning authorities tried to force them to hand over their adopted daughter, Xiao Yanzi, whom they found abandoned in the winter of 1991. The family was a large one, with four older children in the household, ranging in age from ten to thirty-five in 1991. The father,[30] known as Lao (old) Ding, and the mother, Huang Xing (who was blind from birth), were in their fifties when Lao Ding found an abandoned baby early on a cold February morning by the gate of a hospital where he was visiting a sick friend. She was a newborn, with her umbilical cord still attached. Lao Ding's first thought was that the infant would die from the severe cold, so he quickly wrapped her in his coat and took her home. Upon closer inspection at home they could see that she was yellow from jaundice and seemed unwell. So they took her back to the hospital for treatment even though they were poor and it was difficult for them to afford the medical fees. After nursing her through several bouts of illness for three or four months, local officials became aware that they had picked up a foundling and apparently intended to adopt her. Because Ding and Huang had birth children, they could not legally adopt a foundling, so birth planning officials showed up at their home to take the child from them. When Lao Ding refused, the local officials said the family would have to pay a fine of 6,000 yuan, from a yearly family income that was less than half that. Ding remembers saying, "You might as well ask us for one hundred thousand, we can't possibly find enough money to pay you. We are poor and have already spent all of our money to save this child's life! She will die if you take her and put her in an orphanage, she is sickly and needs lots of care." He argued angrily that it would cost the government money to take her; they should be grateful to Ding and Huang for saving them the expense instead of coming to harass them and ask them for money. He finally declared before pushing them out the door, "We intend to keep her as our daughter." Lao Ding was a small, wiry man, but you could see he was stubborn and that he knew how to argue. Although many friends and relatives urged them to give up the baby in the face of this pressure, including their eldest son, the couple stubbornly refused. Birth planning officials came again and again to pressure them, to try to take the child away, but Lao Ding stood firm. Huang Xing recalled clutching the child firmly in her arms during these visits, begging to be allowed to keep the child. Apparently, forcibly taking a child from the arms of a blind woman was a step too far for these local officials. Finally, after months of harassment, the head of the local women's federation intervened on behalf of Huang Xing, arguing that three of their birth children were grown and would soon leave home to work outside the area and within a few more years their youngest daughter would marry and also move away. Huang Xing was blind, and when the baby grew up she could help Huang and Ding as they got older. Only after a fierce argument did the local officials finally relent and let them keep the girl, eventually allowing the family to buy her a local hukou.

Now in her twenties, the first in her family to graduate from high school and go to college, Xiao Yanzi expresses a fierce loyalty to the parents who struggled to keep her and support her through all of these years despite the obstacles and opponents who stood in their way, even deflecting the opposition of their eldest son, her "Dage" (oldest brother), whom she still resents. Nonetheless, she says she is polite to him, finding that her best revenge is to do well and show him how wrong he was when he argued against her joining the family. Working for a company in Suzhou, she returns to see them every few months and sends them a portion of her salary, particularly important now that the government has taken the family's land, paying them barely enough rent to buy a sufficient amount of grain for the old couple. She is a good filial daughter, fully incorporated into a large family of older siblings and same-age nieces and nephews, still living together with some of them in her parents home.

This was our first glimpse of how birth planning and adoption regulations tried to suppress local adoption, even when it seemed cruel and irrational on all sides to do so. As Lao Ding pointed out, to seize the baby would cost the government money and would endanger her life. Here they were, a poor farming family, willing to care for this child with all of their meager resources and energy. How could the government, with no good place to put her, take her from them? Would they rather she die? Lao Ding said the local orphanage was a shambles at the time, with virtually no staff or resources capable of caring for a sick infant. Nor was there any hint of international adoption at the time to incentivize local officials to take the child in order to obtain high adoption fees, an issue that emerges much later. Years later, Lao Ding still shakes his head as he recalls the events of this time.

Over the years, we learned of many cases of official efforts to

fine adoptive parents for "overquota adoptions" of foundlings or
to seize the adopted child from them. In none of these cases did officials even consider the welfare of the child but rather legitimized
their actions as enforcement of government birth planning restrictions reinforced by the adoption law. If the child was damaged in the
process, it seemed to mean little to those tasked with enforcement.
Certainly there was nothing in the letter of the law that put the
interests of the child ahead of restricting the adoption of an out-of-
plan child.

It was particularly difficult to get away with an adoption in urban areas other than an official one from a state orphanage. In a typical case, an urban woman living in a large southeastern city with her
husband and a seven-year-old son took in an infant girl found by her
mother outside a city hospital in the early 1990s. She immediately
got the local police to certify that the child was abandoned so she
could not be accused of an overquota birth and she could prove that
the child was truly a foundling who had no one to take care of it. Unfamiliar with the adoption law, she thought this would be enough to
protect her and the baby. But after raising the child for nearly a year,
the neighborhood birth planning office found out she had adopted
the baby and went to her house insisting she immediately take the
child to the orphanage. She showed them the police certificate and
argued with them to no avail. They told her the police certification
that the child was abandoned was irrelevant; she did not qualify
to adopt because she already had a son; besides, foundlings had to
be given to the government. When the officials got a car to take
the child to the orphanage, the adoptive mother insisted on going
with them and got into the back seat of the car with the child in
her arms. Her mind raced as she tried to think of a way to escape.
When the car stopped at a light, she pushed the door open and
jumped out with the baby. She recalled that the person sitting next
to her seemed to have some sympathy for her plight because he let

her overwhelm him though he was much stronger than she. From that day, she ran from birth planning officials, finding friends in a rural area who helped hide her baby. Whenever she heard about a birth planning drive, she would disappear with her daughter again, leaving her son and husband at home to deal with the officials who came looking for the overquota adopted daughter. When the girl reached school age, the adoptive mother had to arrange for her to live with a close friend and go to a village school where a hukou was not required. Her friend told the teachers that the child was a niece who was staying with her because her sister was ill. Nonetheless, the adoptive mother missed her daughter and periodically tried to bring her home. This cat-and-mouse game went on for most of the girl's childhood. Finally when the girl was twelve, during a government drive to register unregistered hidden children before an upcoming local census, the adoptive family managed to pay a fine and buy her a hukou as a nonfamily member living in their household. This was a hard-won victory that had cost everyone a great deal, straining relations between the mother and father as well as with their son who was often fending for himself. The mother remained unhappy that her child could not be acknowledged as their daughter on the household register.[31]

Sometimes even legally qualified adoptions had to be defended from birth planning officials' efforts to take away an adopted child. One adoptive father[32] living in a small city in the 1990s found an infant boy with a cleft palate abandoned outside the hospital where he worked as a surgeon and decided to adopt the baby and get him the medical treatment he needed. After multiple surgeries, the child was healthy, active, and bore only a small scar on his lip when we met them. The adoptive parents said that birth planning officials had challenged their adoption of the boy on several occasions, threatening to take him away because the couple already had two young adult children, a son and a daughter, both of whom loved their little brother dearly. As a result the parents always carried a copy of the 1991 adoption law as well as several pages of medical records proving that their adopted son was found with a life-threatening disability. The adoption law, well worn and carefully underlined, showed that an abandoned disabled child could be legally adopted by parents who did not meet the standard age or childlessness requirements demanded of other adopters. One official tried to argue that since the boy was now healthy the adoption was illegal! Thus the parents had to be vigilant in protecting the child's and their own rights against efforts to take their son and remove his hukou from their family.

We also learned of many successful efforts by the government to take children from adoptive parents, sometimes forcibly. A bachelor living with his mother in a village told us how in the early 2000s a group of birth planning officials came to his house, overpowered him, and took his one-year-old adopted daughter despite his protests and a later petition to a local court arguing that he and his mother qualified as an adoptive family with the means to raise the child, a petition that he lost. He and his mother later adopted another girl, who was ostensibly found "abandoned" but actually was secretly given to him by birth parents who wanted to hide an unregistered birth of a third daughter and knew the adoptive father had a previous child taken from him. Thus he got another chance to be a father, and the birth parents successfully hid an out-of-plan birth. Had he paid the parents for the child? He insisted he had not, aside from a small *lijin* (gift) to thank them, but he had paid officials tens of thousands of yuan for his daughter. This time, wiser from his bitter past experience, he managed to obtain a hukou through *guanxi* (connections) and numerous bribes. He was a skilled carpenter with a higher than average income so he could afford to pay off officials to preempt them. He told us he was not afraid that this child would be taken. He said, "I have talked to local officials. I told them if they took another child from me, I would kill them. I am a bachelor;

without my daughter, I will have no family and nothing to lose. They know what I say is true and won't dare come again." Being a father was more important to him than anything else in his life, including his freedom. The fact that he had managed to get his adopted daughter a hukou, though as an unrelated person in his household, probably protected her as much as his murderous threats. She was no longer an unregistered child and could not be so easily seized.

Sometimes unregistered children were taken away after being raised by adoptive families for many years; the children themselves might even be unaware they were adopted, assuming they were born into their families. In 2010, when visiting a foster care complex attached to a state orphanage in a small city near the Yangzi River, I met a nine-year-old girl who had entered the orphanage two years earlier. We wondered how a healthy child at that age had ended up in the orphanage. An orphanage official explained that the girl had been taken away from a local adoptive family who came to them in 2008 asking for help in obtaining a hukou so their daughter could go to school. The adoptive parents came forward because they had heard of a new reform policy to give hukou to unregistered adopted children, a known problem in that area. The parents were horrified when told they were not qualified for the amnesty in this reform because they had a son when they adopted their daughter as a foundling and, furthermore, now that the officials knew of this situation, they could not keep their illegal unregistered daughter any longer. The orphanage official told us this girl was "like a birth child" to her adoptive parents, having raised her "as if their own" for seven years; they were naturally devastated by this horrible turn of events, and the child was profoundly distraught for many months. The official felt deeply sorry for the parents and the child. Nonetheless, the officials "had to follow the law," a law that she said had been implemented very strictly in recent years in order to support the one-child principle. Her hands were tied. The adoptive family was allowed to visit occasionally, but the child would likely spend the rest of her childhood as a ward of the orphanage. Although her papers had been sent to the central adoption authorities in Beijing, making her available for an international adoption (domestic adoptions are processed locally), they thought an adoption was unlikely at her age. Furthermore, they doubted the child would consent to being adopted, especially to a foreign country, as was required by orphanage regulations when a child turned ten years old.[33] When a friend visited the orphanage two years later, the girl was still living there and said she did not want another family and did not want a foreigner to adopt her. She was happier now living with her friends in the orphanage. We did not find out if she was still seeing her adoptive family. It seemed cruel to ask her, and the friendly orphanage official was not available.

In a similar case, a US adoptive family discovered shortly after returning home from China that the seven-year-old girl they had just adopted from a large state orphanage in a major eastern city was the daughter of a local Chinese family that the girl expected to rejoin after a short stay in the orphanage, arranged in order to get her a hukou so she could attend school. Fortunately, the child knew her home phone number, and her new US adoptive mother, who spoke some Chinese, was willing to try it. When reached by phone, the Chinese parents, weeping but greatly relieved to know where their "disappeared" child was, confirmed her story. Her Chinese parents said they had found her as a newborn and for seven years had been unable to register her in their family because they had an older son. Even under the best of circumstances, big city hukous were almost impossible to obtain. Although they were relatively wealthy, they told us later when we met them that they had been unable to buy a hukou for any amount of money or bribe someone to get one. Thus they put their daughter in the orphanage in order to try to legalize their adoption and get her an urban hukou so she could register for school and become a legal person in the world. They thought the orphanage director, whom they paid to provide room and board for their daughter, had agreed to this arrangement, but instead she soon placed the child in an international adoption, telling the Chinese parents much later that their adoption could never be legalized because they had an older son and they had raised her illegally for seven years. At the time their daughter disappeared, no one at the orphanage would tell them what had happened to her or where she had gone. They were frantic and heartbroken. The girl, totally confused, wanted to return to her family in China, feeling as if she had been kidnapped. Fortunately, the US adoptive parents, defying US adoption agency recommendations and all legal advice, eschewed their legal power to prevent any contact with the previous family because they felt this was against the needs of their child and also unfair to her Chinese family who loved her deeply. Because they helped her reconnect and maintain contact with her Chinese family, this adoptee, now a young adult, has been able to integrate both families into her life, spending summer vacations with her Chinese family since she was a teen. This was a rare case where the damage done by Chinese government policies and its officials was significantly mitigated by the efforts of the parents on both sides of the Pacific.

In our research we learned directly about more than a dozen children adopted to the United States from state orphanages in the 1990s and early 2000s who came into the orphanage after being taken away from adoptive families in China. Similar cases have been recorded in documentary films about adoption from China[34] and can be found in cases detailed on Chinese Internet forums. International adoptive parents and adoptees searching for birth parents in China, a trend that is increasing rapidly,[35] have also reported finding out that their child was taken from a Chinese adoptive family by the government and placed in an orphanage for another adoption. In some cases, the Chinese adoptive family had been carefully chosen by the birth parents, who were later dismayed to learn the adoptions had been disrupted and their child was now missing; in several documented cases, the birth parents, upon learning the child was seized by officials from the adopters, tried unsuccessfully to retrieve their child from the orphanage. As we learned from birth parents who relinquished children, knowing where the child was and knowing from afar how she was doing in her adoptive family was important to birth parents' peace of mind. The Chinese adoptive families who lose children in this way, like birth parents, report sadness and loss that lasts many years even if they had raised the child for only a few months. One adoptive mother said they felt as if "their own child" was taken from them and that she was so distraught she did not leave her bed for over a month. Not allowed to see or even inquire about the child's whereabouts, they worried for years about what had happened to "their daughter," until many years later the international adoptive parents came to the village searching for the adoptee's birth parents, providing an enormous sense of relief that their former child was happy and well.[36]

It is unclear what proportion of children entered state orphanages in this way. Nonetheless, these cases suggest that "abandoned children" were not necessarily brought in from the streets and roads, but often were taken from families by local officials or the families were pressured to hand the child over to authorities under threat of a heavy penalty. When children were taken, adoptive parents were sometimes named as "finders" on the orphanage documents that were required for entering a child into the orphanage, labeling the child "abandoned," and thereby making it available for another official adoption.

This route into the orphanage and into an officially sanctioned adoption fits neither the image of the "unwanted abandoned baby" found unattended in a public space or the trafficked child purchased from profit-seeking baby-sellers or "rescued" from "buyers," a term currently used by the government and media to describe de facto adopters. Perverse incentives to use birth planning regulations and power for financial gain, public or private, may of course be part of this official behavior, as we shall see in other cases below, but the immediate rationale for taking children of "unclear origins" was to uphold the government's birth planning regulations and the national adoption law. We will see in the next case how local officials periodically came under great pressure to improve birth planning work, which includes preventing or eliminating out-of-plan children living in their jurisdiction. Unregistered adopted children are prime targets because adoption regulations provided the means and the legal cover to accomplish this goal. Notably, the interests of the child do not emerge in any interviews with officials or those involved in removing illegal children from families, regardless of the self-evident trauma suffered by the child.

Under the regularized surveillance and administrative measures of the 2000s, hiding an unregistered adopted child may have become more difficult in some areas. Hiding one's out-of-plan birth child from authorities also put that child at risk of being taken as a "found child" or illegally adopted child, a risk that appears to have increased whenever local areas were put on notice to improve their birth planning records or else suffer demotions, fines, and loss of jobs, as happened in various areas of central and central south China, such as Anhui, Hunan, and Guizhou. This was painfully illustrated for us by a case that we stumbled upon in 2008.

"The Sky Fell Down": The Government Kidnaps "Victory," a Hidden Daughter

In summer 2008, my colleague Wang Liyao and I visited a small village a few hours outside a provincial capital looking for a man named Xu Guangwen,[37] whom we heard "may have abandoned a child" in 2005. Curiously, he was listed as the "finder" of an abandoned baby on the police report that accompanied a child that was taken to a nearby state orphanage and later sent into an international adoption.[38]

As we have seen, outright abandonment had declined in this area and by 2005 was becoming rare. In our research from 2008 to 2012, using the same networks and methods we used so successfully in the 1990s, it was hard to find more than a few cases in this wide area of formerly high numbers of abandonment. Some of the few cases we found turned out to be staged or otherwise fabricated "abandonments" manufactured by birth parents and adopters together for the sake of covering the identity of the birth parents and making the child available for a legal locally registered adoption as a foundling, something that was possible in this area from around 2001 to 2011, when all legal adoption channels outside state orphanages were closed down by regulations from Beijing. So we pursued this possible case hoping to find out the circumstances and reasons for a recent abandonment. Everything we heard about this case was unusual in our past experience in this area. It was said that the family already had a son and that the abandoned child was the family's first daughter. In our previous research we found that the vast majority of abandoned or secretly adopted-out girls in this area had one or more sisters but no brothers. Why would someone who already had a son abandon their firstborn daughter, even if overquota, rather than find a way to hide her or pay for her as so many others did in these villages? Given the popular culture in this area, a girl would likely be a welcomed outcome of a second birth in a daughterless family. We had just recently talked to a number of parents in this province who had a second birth after having a son in the expressed hope of having a daughter, fully aware that the fine would be very high if the overquota child was discovered and that they would eventually have to pay a great deal to register the child, regardless of how or when they did it. These parents were pleased nonetheless, remarking that "it was worth it," and reiterating the "traditional" saying, "A son and a daughter make a family complete." There must be something unusual for someone with a son to proceed with an overquota pregnancy and then abandon the child because it was a girl.

So what had happened? What circumstances shaped this case? Was it an unintended pregnancy that for some reason they, like Wanru, were unwilling to abort even though they had decided they could not keep the child in the face of the penalties? Was there an unexpected family crisis? We started out with many questions about this unusual pattern—a family with a son abandoning their first daughter—wondering if in fact this man really abandoned his daughter at all. Rumors are often wrong. Perhaps it was a false claim to establish a relationship with the internationally adopted child's adoptive parents, although this too seemed unlikely in our experience.

When we first entered the village, we spoke with the current township (*xiang*) head, who immediately remembered this case. He lowered his voice, as if to speak confidentially, and said that Xu Guangwen "had no choice" but to give up his overquota daughter. When pressed for details, he told us how to find Xu's home so we could ask him ourselves what had happened. He told us that Xu lived in a tiny hamlet called Xujiakou with other members of the extended Xu family.

Having "no choice" was a common expression used by birth parents that abandoned babies in the 1990s; though heartfelt, it was rarely literally the case; even a highly "coerced choice" involved a choice of sorts. "Had no choice" (*meiyou biede banfa*) meant the choices were difficult, that they were hemmed in, that they faced destruction of their home and their livelihood if they kept the child, that given their need to have a son they could not afford to get caught with this baby girl and submit to sterilization as was often mandated even after a permitted second birth. There was also often an element of rushed panic in the decisions that were made, leading people to feel they truly "had no choice." So "had no choice" usually referred to the difficult circumstances and limited, costly choices the birth parents faced due to the birth planning policies in their area at that time. We certainly knew by now that these relinquishments were not "voluntary" in any meaningful way even if they represented a coerced choice.

When we arrived at Xu's house, he came from across the road on his motorcycle to meet us, a good-looking man in his late thirties wearing khakis and a white short-sleeve shirt. He had already gotten word that we were coming and had rushed back to meet us. We walked into a courtyard where there were several children playing with a kitten, and an elderly grandmother and a younger woman in a separate enclosed kitchen area cooking lunch. After we talked for a while, Xu told us the story of his out-of-plan overquota daughter and what lead to her "abandonment."

Xu, the fourth of five sons, and his wife Jiang Lifeng's firstborn child in 1994 was a boy. Both parents were happy to have a son although also a bit disappointed that they would now be unable to have a second permitted birth. Jiang especially wanted to have a daughter someday. Although birth planning was tight in the early 1990s, they hoped that things would loosen in time as it had in the past. Two of Xu's older brothers had managed through various machinations to have overquota births in the mid-1990s, and they had children of both genders. Xu's second oldest brother had a son and then two years later had an overquota daughter, for which they paid a moderate fine of 1,000 yuan when discovered in 1996. The third older brother had three daughters before finally having a son, sending the third of the three daughters away in a secret adoption while hiding the second daughter in her maternal grandmother's home until after his son had been born. He paid a 5,000 yuan fine retrospectively when officials discovered he already had two (actually three) daughters at the time the boy was born. He also had to spend over 5,000 yuan to get his second daughter a local hukou, which recorded her as a "relative" from a nearby area.[39]

Thus Jiang and Xu had reason to hope they too would be able to find a way someday to have another child, a daughter if they were lucky. Nine years later when Jiang got pregnant again, birth planning in their area was not only tight but much more regularized and efficient than it was in the 1990s. Every fertile married woman was supposed to have a pregnancy test four times per year to make sure there were no out-of-plan pregnancies in progress. If discovered, abortion was mandated by local regulations. If someone managed somehow to have an out-of-plan birth, not only was the fine high but the mother would also be required to undergo sterilization, and the parents might lose their house. In those years, known overquota births were relatively few but when discovered were treated harshly. Thus when Jiang found out she was pregnant in the spring of 2003, she had to think of a way to hide it. With the help of a friend, she faked her pregnancy tests by secretly bringing her friend's fresh urine to the test. She stayed as thin as she could without endangering her health and the pregnancy, and in the last few months of the pregnancy she went to her mother's home in a neighboring province and stayed inside until she gave birth. Had she been caught at any time during the pregnancy, she would have been forced to abort the baby and would have been sterilized. Jiang was relieved and thrilled when she finally gave birth to a baby girl in early 2004 at her mother's home. The baby was small but otherwise very healthy. Because Jiang's own health had been compromised by her ordeal to hide her pregnancy, she was not able to produce enough milk to feed her daughter for more than ten days, but the baby thrived nonetheless.

Jiang recalls that her infant daughter had a perfect oval face, with pure white skin and full rosy pink cheeks. And she had her mother's dimples. She was everything Jiang had ever hoped for. Both Jiang and her husband agreed the baby would take her mother's surname Jiang and the Xu family generational name as part of her given name. Because of the long and difficult struggle Jiang had endured to give birth to this child, she named her Shengshi, *sheng* meaning "victory," and *shi* meaning a "gentleman or scholar," a name indicating the child's generational rank in the Xu family, a name she shared with her older brother and all of her cousins. But everyone called Jiang's daughter "Baobei," precious baby.

When the baby was a month old and thriving, Jiang returned to her home in the village. The birth planning situation in their village was very strict, and they heard that in addition to fines, houses were again being torn down for violations. They were fearful that their family "would cease to exist in this village," named after their ancestors, both literally and figuratively, if the subterfuge of hiding this birth was discovered at that time. Later, things might improve. So Jiang and her husband agreed that, if asked, they would say Lifeng had found the baby while working outside and brought her home because she could find no one else to take care of the baby. Jiang and Xu knew it was illegal for them to give birth to another child, but they did not think that it was so serious to take in a helpless, abandoned baby found on the road. They clearly were not familiar with the adoption law and the regulations surrounding "found" children. They assumed they would eventually find a way to get a hukou for Jiang Shengshi in their family, like the other brothers had done with their overquota children. It would just take time and money. It never occurred to them that their daughter could be taken from them in the meantime.

Unfortunately, times had changed. The new head of birth planning in the township was under great pressure from above to improve the birth planning record in this area. It had been among the worst in the county for many years. Under the "one vote veto rule" all the officials had been held back or punished for this. He was sent to the area to turn the situation around and immediately set to work cracking down on out-of-plan births and ridding the area of "illegal" children before the next upper-level evaluation in 2005. The village head told us that even minor infractions, such as the failure to discover and report an unauthorized pregnancy early in its gestation, could result in a local official having part of his or her salary docked. Indeed, this happened to him three times since becoming village head, costing him nearly half of his salary in one year. As part of the effort to clean up birth planning work, the township office offered a 2,500 yuan reward for anyone providing information about over-quota pregnancies or hidden children in the area, promising that the identity of the tipster would be kept anonymous.

Shortly thereafter, someone informed on Xu and Jiang. Sheng-shi was nine months old and spent every day with her parents, who took turns caring for her inside the house, rarely taking her very far outside for fear of being seen. Around noon one day in September, seven men approached their home from different directions. Xu was home with the baby, who was asleep in their bedroom. Jiang, working in a nearby field, saw the men approach from all sides and came running in a panic, just in time to see the men push their way into their bedroom and pick up the sleeping baby, carrying her off to a waiting van. As they left the house, Jiang said she "felt the sky fall down" on her as she staggered after them, shocked and aghast at what had just happened. When she reached the van several paces behind them, they let her in to ride with them to the township birth planning office. Xu pursued the van to the office on his motorcycle. What ensued was an eight-hour ordeal of weeping and pleading to get their baby back from the men, a standoff with Jiang and Xu refusing to let them remove the baby from their arms and the men refusing to allow the couple to leave the office with their baby as several men blocked the door. At the outset, Xu offered to pay the highest current fine for an overquota child, which was 10,000 yuan in his village. If they wanted more, he would find a way to get more money from his friends and relatives and double that, he said. However much they wanted, he would find it. He was told that "no fine would be enough" for them to keep this child; she was an "illegal" child in their family, and she could not stay in the village. This area had to be cleared of illegal children. Nothing would change this.

Jiang's mind was a blur; how could they take her daughter! She never imagined something like this could happen. The officials said they knew the child was found somewhere outside the village because Jiang was not pregnant the previous year. They had the records to prove it. In order to prevent her unborn baby from being aborted, she had lied, and now her lie was being used to take her daughter from her. For the first time Jiang realized that she was trapped and would not be allowed to keep this "found" child. There was no way to persuade them and escaping with the baby was not an option. Her knees buckled, and she fell to the floor as Xu looked on helplessly, holding their baby. She lay there for a long time, weeping and begging "without any face." Finally, the men allowed two of her relatives into the room to talk to her as the officials sent for a car to take the baby to the state orphanage in the provincial capital that night. Her relatives, as unfamiliar with the law and their rights as Jiang and Xu, calmed her by saying they would be able to get the child back after she was placed in the orphanage. Then they could find a way to make the child "legal" in their family. If they could not do it themselves, they would send some relatives to adopt her for them. Definitely there would be a way. Finally, Jiang quieted; convincing herself that she could get her daughter back before too long, she resigned herself to the fact that the men were going to take Shengshi that night regardless of how much she begged. They had overwhelming force to impose their will, which did not waver during eight hours of crying and pleading and offering money.

The officials offered two ways of taking the child to the orphanage. One way was to secretly abandon the child near the gate to the orphanage just before dawn. The other way was the "legal way," to formally deliver the baby with signed and sealed papers saying that Xu had found this child in his fields that night. Xu would go with them to the orphanage to certify that this was a true statement. Of course Xu chose the latter method, unable to bear the thought of the officials putting his baby down on the street, leaving her vulnerable and alone to be found at some undetermined time. So he signed the "finder's papers" affirming that what the official papers said was true, that he had just found this baby that night in his fields and did not know who had put her there.

He returned home several hours after midnight, physically and emotionally exhausted. Neither Xu nor Jiang slept the rest of the night. As morning approached they went to the orphanage to ask to adopt the child that had come in last night. They said in fact she was their child, and they had raised her for nine months. The staff at the gate would not let them inside. They were told they could not adopt that child; even if they were qualified to adopt a child from this orphanage, they would have to apply and stand in line to adopt another child assigned to them by the orphanage. This could take years. This failed attempt by Jiang and Xu was followed by two attempts to send relatives to adopt their child. But neither relative was successful. They were also told that no one can choose a particular child and that if they were qualified to adopt, there was a waiting list of at least two to three years. Alas, all was lost. Short of breaking into the orphanage and stealing their baby, there was no way they would ever get her back. The government had taken their baby, stripped them of their parental rights, and left them heartbroken and powerless to do anything about it. It had been nothing short of a kidnapping by the government, leaving them with no recourse.

For many months, Jiang was barely able to eat or speak and cried day and night. Her family feared for her health and sanity. At night she would dream that her child was back with her, that her life was happy and normal; then she would wake with a gasp, realizing that the reality was a nightmare. It took Jiang almost three years to "calm her heart" and go on. She had a wonderful son and a husband and needed to find life again. But her heart would always have a huge hole in it; Jiang Shengshi, her Baobei, would never leave her mind. Whenever she saw a little girl about the same age, she would cry silent tears, and once again her heart would ache.

For a long time she didn't know what had happened to her daughter. She thought of how horrible this separation must have been for Shengshi, who was suddenly ripped from her parents who had been with her every day of her life. As a mother, these thoughts were searing. Even worse, she blamed herself for failing to protect her daughter, failing to foresee and somehow find a way to avoid what befell them. Although she did not know where her daughter was for over a year, she assumed that some family had adopted her, either in China or abroad. She comforted herself with the thought that since it was both difficult and expensive to adopt a child from the orphanage, the adoptive parents would be people who really wanted her and would be good to her and give her a good life. Xu also suffered for a long time from the loss of his daughter. He said that every time he drives by the township offices, his stomach churns as he remembers that horrible day they were held in that office and their daughter was taken from them. He tries to avoid that route whenever possible. It was the very worst day of his life, one that left him feeling drained and powerless, one he could not forget.

When Xu and Jiang learned that their daughter was adopted abroad, that she was an only child in an economically secure middle-class family that loved her and could care for her, they were greatly relieved but also disappointed that she was taken so far away that they might never be able to see her again. Even though the adoptive parents had searched for them, allegedly the "finders," in order to learn more about their daughter's origins, they were shocked by the truth of what had happened and were not immediately willing to bring their daughter to see them as Jiang had initially hoped. After exchanging a few letters contact lapsed and became infrequent. Jiang Lifeng still hoped someday the adoptive parents might change their minds and bring their daughter to China so she could see her in person and tell her that her birth parents loved her, always wanted her, and did not abandon her. She wanted her daughter to know that the day she was born was a day of great joy for her parents who hoped to see her grow up to be a young woman. But Jiang, mindful of the need for stability in her daughter's new life, said she would never want to do anything to disrupt the family she now knew and loved, that she would never do anything to disrupt her life and family again. Her requests of the adoptive parents were minimal, for contact and an occasional visit so her daughter could know them. But this rural couple was nearly as powerless in the face of the international adopters as they were before their own government. This was a bittersweet ending that reignited the tears and nightly dreams of loss for many months, leaving us, especially my colleague, feeling complicit in their suffering. Nonetheless, it was much better for them knowing their daughter was well and had adoptive parents that loved her than never knowing for sure what had happened to their daughter. The latter would have ruined their lives.

Xu Guangwen and Jiang Lifeng's emotionally wrenching story poignantly illustrated how both birth planning and adoption policies created excruciating vulnerabilities for children who are born "out of plan" and remain unregistered. Above all, the case shows how in this area local officials were politically incentivized to seek out and remove such children. They avoided loss of salary and consolidated their political positions, earning a high rating for their performance in the crucial area of birth planning work. The financial incentive of collecting a high fine from Xu and Jiang was irrelevant to them in this context, so they refused Xu's plaintive pleas to take money instead of the child.[40] The financial incentive came in the form of higher political rank and the bonuses that might accompany a good record under the "one vote veto rule."

While the birth parents in this story suffered incredibly, the hidden child also lost everything she had, even if she fortunately went on to find a good life with a new family. At nine months, she was stripped of her identity; she had her parents, brother, extended family of grandparents, uncles, and cousins, and her birthright as a Chinese citizen taken from her by local government birth planning officials whose only concern was to clear their record of an overquota child, a child that had no right to exist in their area. Shengshi was no doubt traumatized by the horrible events that landed her in a state orphanage where she spent over a year of her life while her papers were processed to send her out of the country, being cared for by strangers in an institutional setting before being handed off again to strangers who took her to a distant and unfamiliar land. However resilient a young child may be, this was not a good way to begin a life. She will grow up outside of China perhaps believing, according to the dominant discourse on Chinese adoption, that she was abandoned by Chinese parents who did not want her because she was a girl, even though, on the contrary, they struggled to keep her and gave her a name that means "victory" and "surpassing a gentleman," the daughter of a strong woman who risked everything to give her life, and then lost everything in the gambit. Indeed, how could any young child, or even young adult, come to terms with being kidnapped by the government and thrown into an orphanage without being retraumatized and hurt further after she has managed to find another secure life. While it may be better than imagining one was "abandoned," it is a harsh and challenging truth to absorb. The damage imposed on all by these heinous acts can never be undone.

Like other out-of-plan children who were confiscated from families, "Victory" was among the dwindling number of healthy children in a large state orphanage that had been conducting international adoptions for over a decade. This orphanage was designated a model. Although, as we will discuss below, some orphanages made efforts to draw in more healthy children during this period by working with networks of finders and increasing finder's fees, there is no evidence that this orphanage ever did this. After a notable spike of abandonment and probably the removal of illegal adoptions from families around the 2000 census, as local birth planning officials throughout the area scrambled to get their birth numbers within quotas, this orphanage saw the numbers of healthy infants steadily decline to a handful a year by 2005, although the numbers of "special needs" children remained high. In this area where customary adoption was common, there was finally a system put in place in the early 2000s to allow those local adoptions that fit the law to be legally registered outside the orphanage, thereby allowing the local population to absorb more of the declining number of healthy "abandoned" children that might be found in the city and surrounding counties. In the case of Xu and Jiang's child, we could find no evidence that any money had crossed hands at any point, aside from the significant political and financial incentive created by establishing a clean birth planning record for local officials under the "one vote veto rule." The orphanage, of course, received the designated $3,000 donation for the adoption, entirely legal and agreed to by both governments. While international and some Chinese media construe similar cases as rooted in a business of "buying and selling" children, government birth planning policies and the national adoption law created the toxic brew of local official abuse that led to this travesty, all in the name of upholding the legitimate regulations and laws of the state, laws that provide no clear protection for parents' rights or consideration of children's interests within a power dynamic that invites the violation of both.

Although her parents are fortunate to have discovered what happened to their child and are relieved to know she has found a family that loves and cares for her, it is unclear when or if they will ever see their daughter again in person despite their plaintive requests for a visit, a reality that continues to eat away at her parents' hearts. Two governments have legitimized their daughter's adoptive parents' exclusive rights until she turns eighteen, enforced through a legally imposed "clean break" between the child and her previous family, while her birth parents were stripped of any semblance of parental rights, first and foremost by Chinese birth planning practices, then by the adoption laws of China and the receiving country, both signatories of the Hague Convention on international adoption.[41] Though an extreme case, this tragedy illustrates how international adoption, taking place on a terrain of both coercion and enormous inequality between those who lose children and those who gain them, may compound rather than mitigate the human costs created by population policies. In addition to much greater wealth and financial power, those who gain children through this process have the legal power of two governments legitimizing their possession of these children while those who lose them, in addition to being poor, have been dispossessed of any parental rights by the power of their own government and the legal practices of international adoption. In China's international adoption program, all of this takes place in the absence of any reasonable standard of "voluntary relinquishment," under conditions that make it virtually impossible.

The officials who took Xu and Jiang's daughter later defended their actions because their records showed that Jiang was not pregnant that year, so it was impossible that this was her child by birth.

There have been tens of millions of intentionally hidden pregnancies over the last three decades. As we have seen, the elaborate deceptions created to circumvent birth planning policies blur the origins and histories of many children, making it hard for others to know the truth. But my colleague, who interviewed the retired township birth planning official who had ordered that Xu and Jiang's daughter be taken away, read the stony expression on the ex-official's face when confronted with the truth—that the official had ordered Jiang's own birth daughter seized from her arms—as an admission that he knew at the time what he had done. They had taken advantage of the ambiguity of the situation to rid themselves of an over-quota child, a political liability for their record, or, even worse, they had intentionally punished Jiang for her deception as a cautionary tale for others in the villages who might try the same.

Blurred Lines: Stories of Child Confiscation from Gaoping and Zhenyuan

In our research the confiscation of Jiang and Xu's daughter stood out because it involved a forceful removal of a child directly from her birth parents, ostensibly mistaken as an illegally adopted "found child." As we have seen, the adoption law has long been understood to give wide leeway to remove children from unregistered adoptions or any adoption that violated the law; however, removing "illegal" unregistered birth children living with their parents lacked clear authority, although it is also hard to find birth planning regulations or laws that explicitly prohibit this.[42] According to the village head in Xu and Jiang's village, there were four or five other child confiscations in the area in that period, probably just as painful to the parents, but he said the others were, to his knowledge, adopted children, similar to many other cases in our study.[43]

However, Jiang and Xu's case was not entirely unique as the lines between various types of unregistered children were blurred. Media reports caught glimpses of similar dynamics in other areas of rural central south China in the first decade of the 2000s, notably in areas where local officials, like Jiang and Xu's township, had been given "yellow penalty cards" or put on notice for poor birth planning performance,[44] leading local officials to try to reduce or remove out-of-plan children from their jurisdiction. This resulted in officials taking or pressuring the relinquishment of both adopted children and unregistered birth children from their families as the distinction between different types of unregistered out-of-plan children was hopelessly, and sometimes intentionally, obscured. Birth children were rarely taken directly from their own parents, as "Victory" was, but were usually taken from relatives who were fostering them or caring for them while parents were working outside the area. These fostering arrangements looked very much like the temporary hiding arrangements and informal adoptions we saw in our research area. But in a few areas in Guizhou and Guangxi, local officials in this period reportedly asserted more expansively that certain categories of illegal births were subject to removal directly from birth parents, such as births to underage parents outside marriage or unregistered overquota births to poor parents who could not or would not pay the fines. The fact that in the early 2000s there were nearby orphanages that could take in the children and use them to obtain high fees from international adoptions may have allowed more of this behavior to flourish compared to the 1990s, along with tighter local birth planning practices. This confluence of factors revealed an implicit connection between the thirty-year imperative to control births and the "buying and selling" of out-of-plan children, a category of illegal child created by birth planning, a child that is born with a price on its head regardless of who raises it. Coupled with the well-documented ability of local officials to bully poor rural residents, it is hardly surprising that such problems arose.[45]

GAOPING, HUNAN: UNREGISTERED
CHILDREN HELD FOR "RANSOM"

One of the most highly publicized reports of child seizures came from Gaoping town, a poor mountainous area in Longhui County, Hunan, where in March 2006, sixty villagers reportedly filed a protest against birth planning officials, claiming that eleven children had been seized by officials and held for "ransom" in the form of high birth planning fines.[46] According to the investigative report published in Hong Kong's *South China Morning Post*, when the fines could not be paid on the spot, the children were taken to the Shaoyang orphanage, where at least some were reportedly sent into international adoptions before the parents were able to raise the money to pay the fines. Although published in Hong Kong and picked up by papers outside China, the story was squelched in mainland papers until May 2011 when Caixin's *New Century* magazine, in the wake of the release of the 2010 census report,[47] took the story off the shelf and gave it broad coverage for several weeks until it was quashed again.[48] According to Caixin's investigation, all of the children taken by the local officials were unregistered, and all were seized ostensibly as illegally adopted children, which officials said was permitted under the national adoption law. According to the original 2006 report in the *South China Morning Post*, seven of the children were adopted and were without proper registration. Four of the children were reportedly taken from their birth families, three coming from unregistered marriages, the other an overquota birth child. Officials claimed that all of the parents or their relatives who were the caretakers signed papers saying the children were adopted, something disputed by the villagers, some of whom were illiterate and may not have known what they were signing. Some relatives serving as caretakers later told the Caixin reporter that they signed the papers because they were told the fine would be lower for a foundling and that their relative could retrieve the child later when they returned. Whether, when initially confronted, any of these parents or caretakers had presented unregistered children as "found" or "adopted" in an effort to disguise their own or a relative's unregistered out-of-plan birth would not be surprising; as we have seen elsewhere, trying to hide or disguise children's identity was not unusual, as officials should have known. In fact, the officials admitted this could be the case. Hiding children with relatives was also common. Caixin's later and more detailed investigation found at least sixteen children had been taken over a period of a few years, all unregistered, a mix of adopted and birth children, all "out of plan." Most were taken from relatives while the parents were away. Thirteen were sent to the Shaoyang orphanage; only one was returned to the parents after an intervention by a politically influential acquaintance. The returned child was a five-year-old adopted boy whose single father, recently turned thirty, had found and raised him from birth. A sympathetic People's Congress representative was able to reconstruct and gather the paperwork necessary to finally legalize the adoption and pressure officials at the Shaoyang orphanage to return the child after holding him for a month. When the once-happy child was returned to his father, he seemed traumatized by his frightening experience, appearing dazed, unable to speak, and emaciated.[49] The child's father and neighbors were furious to see how the child had suffered but relieved to have him back.

According to Caixin, most of the other children sent to the Shaoyang orphanage were adopted internationally, six reportedly to parents in the United States. Caixin and many of the Longhui parents who lost their children alleged that the children were taken for the purpose of selling them to the orphanage, which reportedly paid local officials 1,000 yuan for each child and then in turn sold the children to international adopters for $3,000 each, the standard orphanage fee at that time charged to all international adopters as mandated by regulations of the Civil Affairs ministry's central adoption authority in Beijing.[50]

Not surprisingly, a Shaoyang government investigation spurred by the Caixin reports found that officials had not taken children illegally for the purpose of selling them to the orphanage and then into international adoption, as the Caixin reporters and the parents alleged. Rather the government report pointed out that the parents had all violated birth planning laws: they claimed one child was handed over by unmarried parents, eight children were illegally adopted (hence subject to seizure under the national adoption law), and the caretaker relatives of five of the children had deceived authorities about the "true origins" and "blood relations" of the hidden, unregistered children, claiming that they were "found children," hence making them subject to removal from the families and relatives by the government because none of them qualified as legal adopters.[51] Hence the parents' deception was blamed; not only had they failed to register their children, but they hid them with other families or relatives. Of course to register the children would have invited unaffordable fines or worse because they were out of plan.

While the government's version was self-serving and did not address the allegation that some of the caretaker signatures had been forged, their "facts," though twisted in places, did not depart radically from the stories told to reporters by parents who lost their children.[52] Inadvertently, the report revealed how expansive birth planning regulations were taken to be and how the power of local officials to implement these was nearly limitless. Almost any out-of-plan child lacking proper registration was fair game. The birth planning law and the behavior it had spawned among parents and officials provided wide latitude for this kind of behavior by local birth planning officials who felt empowered to take "illegal" children, variously defined, and remove them from their jurisdiction, thus improving their own birth planning record and perhaps saving themselves from being fined, all at the expense of largely power-less villagers. Indeed, the system of rewards and punishments under which the local officials operated pressured them to do so. It is worth noting that this system also results in forced late abortions that occasionally surface in the media and on the Internet and would have resulted in the forced abortion of Jiang Lifeng's baby had she been caught before giving birth.[53] A few of the Shaoyang cases appear to have involved pregnancies that were hidden in order to prevent forcible abortions, such as a couple who gave birth to twins in a tent in the forest.

The government report further disputed that the seized children were "sold" to the orphanage, asserting that the international adoptions that resulted were fully legal, and that legal international adoptions could not be characterized as "selling children."[54] Adoption "donations," however high, were reasonable, regulated, and supported the care of the children in the orphanage. Nonetheless, twelve local officials, easy targets for higher-ups as well as reporters, were fired for "severe negligence and for handling work in a simplistic way,"[55] indicating some recognition of the embarrassing public mess that this kind of official behavior had created. However, the manufacturing of "foundlings" out of unregistered children taken directly from birth families or those who were fostering them, children who had not been relinquished, was considered at worst a mistake, one that the birth parents were largely to blame for.[56] Of course, as we have argued, there have been few healthy children in the China adoption program who were truly voluntarily relinquished, including those found abandoned, even if only a minority were directly taken by the government, especially when one considers the vast numbers of Chinese adopters who have lost their children.

While local officials invited censure because they generated an embarrassing public scandal, their behavior was propelled by the official rules under which they operated and survived. As Wang Feng, then director of the Brookings-Tsinghua Center for Public Policy in Beijing, told a *New York Times* reporter, "The larger issue is that the one-child policy is so extreme that it emboldened local officials to act so inhumanely."[57] Although pecuniary incentives may have played a role, local officials could have collected more than the 1,000 yuan they reportedly received from the Shaoyang orphanage simply by allowing the parents time to raise funds to pay off their substantially higher birth planning fines, as was common practice in many parts of rural China. Even poor parents could be expected to come up with more than the 1,000 yuan per child. Such birth planning fines were often used to finance local governments, if not line pockets. What was almost certainly more valuable to local officials in this case was the added benefit of removing the out-of-plan children from their jurisdiction, thus cleaning up their poor birth planning record and avoiding bad marks, demotions, or heavy fines that might be levied against them by higher levels. Trafficking children for profit in these cases is rooted in the perverse incentives, ethos, and regulations that surround birth planning laws and regulations, all of which put out-of-plan children at risk of losing their families, of being shuffled from family to orphanage to another family with no regard for the child's interests or rights, let alone the interests or rights of their parents. Birth planning policies and administrative policies lead to and allow this behavior. In addition, unlike in the early 1990s when local orphanages were ill prepared to care for children who were abandoned or taken from adopters, many orphanages now were set up to do both international and domestic adoptions, so taking in healthy children was hardly a burden as it would have been in the case of Ding and Huang's adopted foundling daughter in 1991. Now a healthy child, born with a steep birth planning price on its head, was a possible source of revenue to an orphanage. With the confluence of these conditions, Gaoping, put on notice to improve its birth planning work, was an example of a "perfect storm."

While Gaoping was a "perfect storm," other such storms were likely to pop up in this climate during this period. A similar case in Zhenyuan County in eastern Guizhou, a province neighboring western Hunan, was brought to light in July 2009 by an extensive investigative report published in *Southern Metropolitan News* (Nanfang Dushi Bao), an independent paper in Guangzhou that published the article in defiance of a prohibition by censors.[58] Another poor area put on notice for its poor birth planning record, local officials had been operating for several years under a local policy that allowed them to take unregistered out-of-plan children from local families in lieu of immediate payment of high birth planning fines. If parents of an overquota child could not pay the fine, they were told they had to turn the child over to the government until they could pay. In the meantime a number of children taken in this way were sent to the Zhenyuan orphanage, where several were then sent into international adoptions. The Zhenyuan orphanage reportedly sent around eighty children into international adoptions between 2001 and 2009, some unknown number of them obtained directly from parents who could not pay the birth planning fines, both adoptive parents and birth parents or relatives who were caring for their unregistered children.

This was the county's official birth planning policy from at least 2003, as stated by one of the local officials who took these overquota children. A Zhenyuan family planning bureau official told *China Daily*, "According to our investigation, it is true that babies who have parents were forced into the orphanage and then abroad." Notably, the local officials did not consider this policy to be contrary to government birth planning regulations until this was suggested to them by the opinion of the *Southern Metropolitan News* investigative reporter. An area in neighboring northern Guangxi is reported to have had a similar policy for many years.[59] Both these areas, like Gaoping, are poor and have relatively high fertility rates, above "policy levels."[60] Indeed, how to handle fines that cannot be paid is not clear in government documents and is largely a matter left to local regulation.[61] Nor as suggested previously are the rights of parents clearly spelled out in the regulations of the birth planning law or anywhere else that we are aware of after many years of studying these issues.[62] Under these circumstances, an official policy that levies fines of two to nine times a family's yearly income, forcing people to pay exorbitantly for the right to raise their out-of-plan children and give them a legal status, leaves room for this kind of official behavior and for much abuse.

In Zhenyuan, the personal angst that some parents suffered from the loss of their children, whether birth children or adopted children, was illustrated by a farmer in Guizhou interviewed by the *Southern Metropolitan News* reporter: "Knife scars around his neck and chest show that Lu Xiande is a human tragedy. He once tried to commit suicide. These knife scars are his special commemoration for his fourth daughter."[63] Farmers in Gaoping tell similar stories of sorrow, rage, impotence, and ultimately resignation in response to having the government take their children and send them out of the country by "selling" them into international or possibly domestic adoption. For a brief period, Caixin reporter Pang Jiaoming reported, a few of the Gaoping fathers plotted to kidnap the children of several birth planning officials, but were persuaded against this disastrous approach.[64]

Media coverage has stressed the similarity between these seizures of out-of-plan children and criminal kidnapping and child trafficking for profit because of the revenue gained from international adoption; similarly, parents have understandably likened birth planning fines to "ransom."[65] The seizure of "Victory" by officials was nothing short of a brutal kidnapping, regardless of local officials' legal cover. Understandably, blaming such blatant disregard of villagers and their children on local corruption and illegal behavior rather than the sanctioned laws of the central government is relatively politically safe and acceptable when the government itself frequently rails against local corruption and has long opposed "illegal human trafficking." Central birth planning policy has been particularly sacrosanct and out of bounds for all but the bravest editors until very recently. Yet as we have seen this local official behavior, as in the case of Xu and Jiang, finds its roots and justification in central birth planning policies and the way they are implemented through high-pressure administrative policies, not primarily or in the first instance in the petty criminal behavior and corruption of local officials. Birth planning fines, in Longhui as elsewhere, were a source of local finance and perhaps personal gain for local officials without removing the children. Many local governments have funded their operations with birth planning fines, something that may or may not be seen as corrupt.[66] Yet Gaoping-Longhui officials preferred in this period to remove the children and forgo the greater sums they might get from fines, just as Xu's offer of 20,000 yuan to keep their daughter was shunned by officials in favor of removing their baby to the state orphanage, an orphanage that to our knowledge did not pay any finder's fees. In at least the cases we have examined, the imperative to remove the child came from pressures generated by the birth planning program and the way it is implemented.

The stepped-up surveillance methods that prevailed in some rural areas in the 2000s, administratively enforced through rewards and punishments meted out to local officials through the "one vote veto rule" (*yipiao foujue zhidu*), created powerful financial and political incentives for local officials to prevent and root out out-of-plan children when this was possible, especially at key times when records are reviewed or the population counted.[67] The usual practice of collecting revenues through fines, leaving the overquota child on the books, may not be enough if a record needs to be cleaned up. As long as officials removed ostensibly "found" or de facto adopted children, or could construe them to be such, they operated under recognized policy and law. In this way, parents' own defensive strategies could be turned against them.

Gaoping, Zhenyuan, and Xu and Jiang's township were areas that reportedly had been put directly under administrative supervision in the early to mid-2000s because of lax records in preventing out-of-plan births. Because unregistered birth children and de facto adopted children are often indistinguishable due to the various ways parents seek to hide out-of-plan children from authorities, officials could use regulations aimed at suppressing domestic adoption to take both unregistered adopted and birth children from their parents or, more often, their relatives. Similarly, requiring parents to pay ruinously high fines for their out-of-plan children has led at least some local officials to interpret official policy as allowing them to take away "illegal" children, even birth children, when fines cannot be paid by poor villagers. Instances of this practice continue up to the present.[68] Although this is not explicitly allowed by central or provincial policies or the birth planning law, one would be hard-pressed to find regulations that explicitly uphold or protect parental rights in the face of birth planning violations and intentional parental deception. After the findings of the Shaoyang government investigation of Caixin's allegations were released, mostly defending the actions of local officials as legal, an editorial by *Economic Observer* perceptively noted the cruel irony of using poor parents' understandable efforts to avoid a harsh policy to justify taking away their children.[69]

CHAPTER 5

An Emerging "Traffic in Children"

While our research indicates the cases of child confiscation that occurred in Gaoping and Zhenyuan were driven primarily by centrally sanctioned birth planning policies carried out by local government officials under upper-level pressure to improve their records in birth planning work, government policies, especially those associated with adoption, did contribute directly and indirectly to behavior that crossed the line into a kind of "child trafficking" involving orphanages, finding parts of the government on both sides. As we have seen, punitive birth planning policies that led parents to hide births filled Chinese orphanages with healthy children in the 1990s. The 1991 national adoption law further contributed to the orphanage population by suppressing customary adoption and removing relinquished children from the population in order to place them under the legal control of the government.

In this context, the introduction of international adoption put in place policies and practices that created incentives that could easily generate a kind of official trafficking, whereby adoptions became a way to raise revenue for state welfare institutions. From its inception in the early 1990s, international adoption fees were used to provide funds for the sorely underfunded child welfare institutions that housed abandoned and orphaned children. Furthermore, as a result of the general financial decentralization of government funding in the 1990s, the local orphanages that did the adoptions were allowed to keep the lion's share of the relatively high fees paid by international adopters. Thus even though the Gaoping and Zhenyuan seizures of children, like the seizure of "Victory," were motivated in the first instance by birth planning pressures, the orphanages that received these healthy children, all three of which did international adoptions, increased their revenues by taking them in. Furthermore, the availability of healthy children was declining in many orphanages even though the international adoption program continued to expand until 2005, reaching almost one-third of all registered adoptions, and the demand for healthy babies was very high. Although the fees paid by domestic adopters were rising, international adopters still paid much higher fees in most places in the early 2000s, a fact that led some orphanages to privilege international adoptions over domestic adoptions even when waiting lists of domestic adopters grew long.[1] In addition to higher fees, international adoptions also brought ties to international nongovernmental organization networks and continuing donations from previous adoptive parents. Thus there were a number of incentives to provide healthy children to international adopters and also to the growing numbers of wealthy domestic adopters.[2]

Orphanages and Their "Finders": The Hunan Trafficking Case on Trial

Under these circumstances, some state orphanages became involved with organized networks of "finders" that brought abandoned or surreptitiously relinquished children from one area to another as orphanages paid escalating "finders fees." Orphanage officials said that this practice began when infant abandonment was high and many people were afraid to pick up babies and bring them to the authorities. Some babies were left to die, according one Hunan official interviewed by a reporter in 2006. Thus reimbursing people for their time and effort was supposed to "encourage people to actively participate in picking up and sending abandoned babies to welfare centers."[3] In our research we found that many people picked up healthy babies without notifying the authorities and adopted them or took them directly to friends or relatives who might want to adopt a child. Almost one-quarter of the adoptive families we interviewed had found the baby on their own doorstep, sometimes reporting this later, sometimes not. From the 1980s on, government policy mandated that all foundlings should be handed over to the government, although local official practice varied, often accepting fines in lieu of the baby. While some people followed this policy and took foundlings to the police, taking a baby to the authorities could cause the finder a lot of trouble. One man who found a sick baby needing hospitalization had to prove that the baby was not his or a close relative's by obtaining a letter from his local birth planning office. Only then was he allowed to drop off the baby.[4] From this perspective, making it easier for people to bring in foundlings and compensating them for doing so could help the government pull foundlings away from customary de facto adoptions as well as save the lives of sick babies who might be left unattended.

Whatever the origins of the practice, when local findings decreased, as they did in central and eastern areas by the 2000s, encouraging extensive networks of finders through employees, relatives, and friends, as the Hunan orphanages reportedly did, could help keep the supply of healthy children steady for state orphanages that did international adoptions, bringing babies in from areas where infant abandonment continued to be high. It is unclear how many orphanages engaged in this kind of active effort to bring in children. But as with the confiscation of certain kinds of children by birth planning officials, these practices not only operated under a cloak of policy and law but were aligned with the purpose of those policies as well—the government's long-standing interest in restricting adoption outside government control. In contrast to most customary adoption practices, the state orphanages' international and domestic adoption programs were legally sanctioned and regulated; the mandatory donation fees they charged both international and domestic adopters were regulated and considered legal. Preventing the surreptitious circulation of out-of-plan children among the local population was a clear government goal ever since the beginning of birth planning efforts. Thus keeping relinquished children away from local adopters and delivering them into government hands for legal adoptions fit larger state policies and goals, not just the pecuniary interests of local orphanages.

Yet, for reasons not entirely clear, the practices of state orphanages in Hunan that brought in children from Guangdong came under scrutiny in late 2005 when a criminal court charged several orphanage directors and a network of their "finders" with "buying and selling children," a criminal offense. Those charged had been caught exchanging several thousand yuan per child by a local police sting operation, perhaps tipped off by another disgruntled orphanage employee who had been cut out.[5] The babies, mostly healthy girls, were originally obtained from a local garbage recycler who, over the years, became known as someone who would take in abandoned babies, take care of them, and pass them off to adopters or orphanages through networks of go-betweens, including orphanage workers.[6] One of the people convicted of trafficking later discussed how the orphanages had steadily increased the amount they "reimbursed" finders from a nominal amount to cover expenses in the mid-1990s when local abandonment was relatively high to several thousand yuan by 2005 when local foundlings were fewer and many, perhaps half, were being brought in from Guangdong.[7]

The timing of the court case coincided with the final implementation of the Hague Convention on international adoption, which prohibits this use of money in the adoption process, although it is not clear if these events were directly connected. Guilty verdicts and jail terms for one of the directors and nine civilians accused of trafficking sent a message that apparently tamped down aggressive orphanage recruitment efforts by these and other orphanages, diminishing further the general supply of healthy children available for adoption through the state orphanage system, including international adoption.[8] Although there continued to be reports of some orphanages paying those who find and bring in babies, one orphanage vice director in a neighboring province told us that he would not even reimburse taxi fare for fear of being accused of "baby buying."

The Hunan court case not surprisingly focused blame on corrupt, greedy local officials and petty criminals, yet the case suggested the ways that the central government itself, under its birth and adoption policies, had become involved in trafficking into international adoption the children marginalized by its population policies. The defendants' insistence that they thought what they were doing was not only in the children's interest but was legal because they were delivering abandoned children to the government, not to criminal traffickers or illegal private adopters, was not unreasonable. Legally sanctioned and criminal behavior were hard to distinguish in part because the underlying dynamics that set them in motion and drew them onto the terrain of buying and selling children were firmly linked to government policies limiting births and suppressing local adoptions in order to prevent parents from circulating hidden out-of-plan children outside of government purview. The convicted traffickers claimed, with good reason, that they were taking abandoned or otherwise relinquished children out of an illegal (de facto) adoption market and placing them into legal government channels for properly credentialed adoption. How could this be illegal trafficking, one asked?[9] Indeed, since official sanction, not the payment of money per se, is the primary criteria for distinguishing "trafficking" from regulated "legal adoption," as seen in the government's defense in the Gaoping-Shaoyang orphanage case, the question was an entirely reasonable one.

"Rescuing the Trafficked Child": Government Discourse on the Adoption Trade in the 2000s

Outside of government channels, the organized buying and selling of children to adopters as a business has also been on the rise since 2000. While this child trafficking business supplied international adoption through paid orphanage "finders," as shown in the 2005 Hunan court case, most of this interregional activity has involved domestic adoption outside of government channels. As we have seen, the suppression of customary, localized adoption practices of the 1980s and 1990s pushed unregistered de facto adoption deep into the shadows as people dodged birth planning regulations in a variety of ways that involved adoption. This made domestic adoption a ready-made market for children brought in from other areas when the local supply of adoptable children dwindled in central and eastern areas of China. In the 1990s, when abandonment was high in our central China research area, the demand for adoption could be met locally by foundlings and by those eager to adopt-out out-of-plan children through various surreptitious methods. But by the 2000s, when abandonment fell in many parts of central and eastern China, a dearth of children, born inside and outside the plan, made itself felt in tight adoption markets. As the adoptive father quoted earlier put it, in the 1990s someone might find an adoptive daughter at their own front door, but a decade later someone could "go out and search and ask everyone they know and still not find a child."

Although legal adoption from orphanages became accessible to a somewhat larger domestic pool of adopters after 1999 when the legal age was lowered from thirty-five to thirty, the number of healthy children in orphanages dwindled significantly over the following decade, making it very difficult for even legally qualified childless Chinese couples to adopt from an orphanage.[10] The difficulty of adopting from state orphanages was exacerbated by the fact that international adoption continued to absorb thousands of healthy children from these institutions throughout the decade, although the numbers of international adoptions also started to decline after 2005. Thus childless Chinese couples who were desperate to find a child to adopt turned to middlemen who operated in the field of unofficial underground adoptions. Many also turned to the unregulated space of the Internet to try to find children that were unavailable through any other means.

Rapid but unequal socioeconomic development and unevenly falling fertility seemed to create perfect conditions for interregional trafficking of children for adoption, usually from poorer areas into richer areas. While fertility fell everywhere, some areas such as Guizhou and Guangxi in the southwest, areas that supplied children for central and eastern China, not only maintained higher fertility levels than eastern and central China but levels that exceeded "policy fertility" by a wider margin than other areas, indicating that there were more "out-of-plan" children in these areas needing to be hidden from authorities.[11] This is the category of children that is most likely to become available for adoption.

As early as 2001, organized networks facilitating domestic adoption in response to the growing shortage in eastern and central China was signaled by the publicized capture and trial of a "ring of child traffickers" from a poor village in Xicheng, Yunnan, near the border of Vietnam.[12] Dozens of villagers were arrested for allegedly smuggling two thousand babies to adopters in eastern China during several years of business. In another case in Yulin, Guangxi, in 2002 a group was caught transporting eleven girls in bags on a long distance bus headed for adoptive families in Anhui. Investigative reports indicated that the Xicheng and Yulin children, like those abandoned or adopted out by birth parents in the 1980s and 1990s, came from the pool of unregistered, hidden children, most of whom were overquota and born "out of plan" to poor peasants who could not afford the fines or who wanted to avoid threatened sterilization. Parents handed them over to middlemen traffickers as a way to hide them. As one such middleman asserted, "There are always people who break the one-child policy and have to sell ... I'm just an agent." He noted that without the policy he would be out of business.[13]

Along with the emergence of unregulated adoption brokers who, like regulated private adoption agencies and adoption lawyers in other countries, earned a profit by bringing adopters together with those who had out-of-plan children they wanted to hide and adopt out, the process of unofficial adoption was vulnerable to the trafficking of kidnapped children as well.[14] The problem of kidnapping has drawn increasing attention from the media and the government, although the latter is often scathingly criticized for inadequate action by those who have lost children to kidnappers.[15] If kidnapped children were sneaked into the mix of children trafficked into adoption, adopters might not even know.

In our research in central rural China, we learned about some of the networks of middlemen that had emerged by the 2000s although not in great depth. From several different sources, we learned about hospital staff involvement in arranging adoptions for birth mothers who wanted to hide the birth of an out-of-plan child. We were told that in this area adoptions arranged through hospital staff cost between 10,000 and 20,000 yuan in 2009, some or all of which went to the birth mother as *lijin*, a kind of ritual gift or payment understood as compensation for her care, the burden of her pregnancy, and perhaps for the risk of fines that she would face if

discovered. This was about the amount that a birth parent would
have to pay the government birth planning office for a first overquota child in this area. We also learned about the existence of
local people who could facilitate connections between would-be
adopters and birth parents who wanted to relinquish a hidden out-
of-plan birth. We were told contradictory things about facilitators,
or those who could find a child to adopt in the area. Several sources
said this would cost at least 20,000 yuan for the birth parents and
facilitator; several others said it would not cost adopters that much
because birth parents needed to find adoptive parents for a hidden
child before it was discovered and those who helped were not running a business but were doing a favor for friends. They said a small
gift, or *lijin*, would usually do. But local people who could facilitate adoptions now seemed as if they might be a ready channel for
trafficking children in from other areas rather than, as in the past,
facilitating the circulation of children through networks of friends,
neighbors, and distant relatives within a local area. However, we
learned little concrete information about children being trafficked
in from other areas, and we learned nothing involving kidnapped
children aside from stories circulating in the media. Yet as unmet
demand surfaced in this area, it was not hard to imagine how these
practices could develop and even flourish there. Given the emerging conditions and the government policies under which they flour-
ished, these various trends involving adoption and child trafficking
predictably increased in parts of the country as China entered the
twenty-first century.

Thus not surprisingly in the 2000s, Chinese police busts of child
trafficking rings have become more frequent and public. Recently,
adoption Internet sites where couples have increasingly turned to
find birth parents relinquishing children, something birth parents
cannot do openly without subjecting themselves to birth planning
punishments and charges of "unlawful abandonment," have also

become subject to police crackdowns. One of these was an adoption website run by an adoptive couple that helped match potential adoptive parents with birth parents and also helped arrange a hukou for the adopted child so that it could enjoy the rights of an "in-plan" child.[16] These crackdowns have brought many "rescued children" into government orphanages, where they are cared for while efforts are made to find their parents. According to police reports, these efforts are usually unsuccessful, at least partly because many of the parents have surreptitiously relinquished out-of-plan children to be adopted and do not want to be found and punished for birth planning violations.[17] In a recent study of around 130 cases of "abduction" reported in the media, a Chinese scholar found that half the cases were children who came directly from birth parents or their relatives and were not kidnap victims.[18] Another report quoted a father who was the "seller" as saying he didn't think relinquishing a child to adoptive parents who would take good care of the child was a crime. Under these circumstances it is unclear what happens to the children. Legally, they must be certified as "abandoned" or orphaned before they are available for international or domestic adoption. Some reportedly wait in institutions for a long time while birth parents are sought.

Crackdowns on trafficking rings also involve taking children away from "buyers," the term now used for the adoptive parents who may already be raising these children, and putting the children into orphanages, in an explicit effort to discourage the demand for these children by forcing the "buyers" to "lose their child and their money," as authorities put it.[19] The latter effort fits well with the long-term government policy of suppression of customary adoption outside government channels and the removal of "illegally adopted" children that accompanied the implementation of birth planning policy. By the end of the first decade of the 2000s, de facto adoption was heavily implicated in what the government considered "child

trafficking" and taking children from adopters now was rationalized as curbing kidnapping and trafficking. The deputy head of the
Ministry of Public Security's criminal investigation bureau, Liu Ancheng, admitted in a news story in 2011 that it was hard to untangle
the web of adoption and trafficking, saying that while many babies
are kidnapped, many more are simply "sold" by parents to adopters.
According to Liu, as reported in an AP story, "the 'dreadful practice
of buying and selling children' is a result of ignorance of the law in
rural areas as well as traditional Chinese social norms that call for
people 'to have both sons and daughters' and for children who will
look after a parent in old age."[20]

Although Liu Ancheng acknowledged a complicated mix of factors involved in "buying and selling" children, a dominant discourse
of child trafficking emerged in media accounts that more often obscured the dynamics discussed above and made invisible the role of
population control and adoption policy. In this discourse, adopters,
except those fortunate enough to be able to adopt from a state orphanage, are dubbed "buyers," those who facilitate adoptions are
called "child traffickers," and the children involved are implicitly,
if not explicitly,[21] assumed to be kidnap victims who must be "rescued" by police from both "buyers" and traffickers and placed in
state orphanages.

Comprehensive crackdowns on child trafficking practices,
whether involving abducted children or those relinquished or
abandoned by their birth parents in order to hide births and avoid
fines, have been widened to include investigations of unregistered
or improperly registered children.[22] As we have seen, many out-of-
plan hidden and adopted children have irregular hukou or none
at all due to the difficulty of registering out-of-plan and adopted
children, as well as the desire of parents to avoid punishment. Any
crackdown on children with irregular or no hukou as an effort to
tamp down trafficking in "stolen children" would inevitably sweep

up many of these children as well. It could be impossible to distinguish kidnapped or "lost" children from de facto adoptions and children being hidden by birth parents. The cases in Gaoping and some of those from Zhenyuan discussed above, in which the local government seized allegedly "illegally adopted" unregistered children and put them in the Shaoyang and Zhenyuan orphanages casts the current government crackdown against "trafficking" and "buyers" in a more ambiguous light, one in which the government itself might be seen as "stealing" or "kidnapping" children from relatives who are fostering them or from adoptive families as well as from traffickers and "selling" them into adoption through state orphanages, accusations made by parents, reporters, and media critics when the Gaoping and Zhenyuan cases came to public attention. The current discourse of child trafficking, in which parents are "buyers" of trafficked "stolen" children, deflects any such critique although some of the same dynamics underlie the phenomena of "child trafficking" and the government response.

The Vulnerability of the Unregistered Out-of-Plan Child: Abandoned, Adopted, Hidden and Trafficked

What ties these cases together is the central role of the "out-of-plan" child, a type of child created by birth planning policy and the categories used to implement it. This is a child whose birth is illegal and whose right to exist as a family member and citizen must literally be purchased from the government by birth parents or potentially by adoptive parents. As we have seen, sometimes even money cannot buy the child's rights. The child is therefore placed in some degree of jeopardy from birth. In a sense, this child's "unclear origins" are officially clarified only through a process of being "bought and sold," a process that may bestow an official, if not always a real, identity. The often ruinously high price in the form of fines, coupled with additional onerous punishments for parents, such as loss of job, loss of property, and sterilization, creates strong motivation for parents, and sometimes local officials, to hide the child rather than "pay the price" for the child, leaving it unprotected by a proper registration that could give the child a clear identity and hence also certain rights, including the right to belong to its family. The lack of registration makes the child an example of "bare life," a human subject "reduced to a naked depoliticized state without official status and juridical rights" unless and until an official identity is bestowed upon them.[23] The origins of millions of Chinese children have become hopelessly obscured by the dynamics of a three-decade-old birth planning policy that has remained fundamentally unchanged in the way it defines and legitimizes only the "in-plan" child that is born with permission and according to the rules and punishes the one that is not. In poor areas where parents cannot afford further impoverishment from government birth planning fines, hidden children and irregular hukou are likely still to be particularly numerous. This is where interregional child traffickers may find their supply. As Wang Li, the adoption middleman in *China's Stolen Children* quoted earlier, pointed out, he would be out of business without this policy, a policy that forces poor people to sell him their unauthorized children. Without this, he would have no supply. And perhaps he would have fewer "buyers" as well.

This trafficking is further fueled by adoption laws making it virtually impossible to openly relinquish a child into a legal adoption, especially an out-of-plan child, making the use of secret adoption networks or abandonment the only routes for poor parents facing destitution from birth planning fines at the hands of the government. Without these birth and adoption policies, poor parents could keep their children without being impoverished by the government or they could relinquish them openly into an adoption, making it easier to isolate and destroy criminal kidnapping gangs while putting the others out of business.

As many of the above cases of government confiscation and child trafficking make clear, the unregistered out-of-plan child is a child at high risk of being victimized by these practices both official and criminal. As mentioned earlier, in our investigation of unregistered "hidden children" without hukou, we found that a disproportionate number of the children who spent time in this category were adopted children and that adopted children were likely to stay in this category longer than others. Lower rates of immunization, lower rates of school attendance between the ages of seven and fourteen, and a range of consequences resulting from increased social stigma are by now well-known consequences of registration difficulties. Perhaps worst of all is the increased risk to a child's secure place in a family. Little Qianqian, who ran and hid in the attic when she overheard her adoptive father and an official talking about entering her into an orphanage for a "brief period" of time as a strategy to get her a hukou, was right to be afraid of such a risky strategy. Had she entered an orphanage to get a hukou, she may never have been able to come home, like several other adopted children we learned about. For two decades, the international adoption pool has been filled with the unregistered, out-of-plan child. On the other hand, registered, in-plan children are highly unlikely to be abandoned, relinquished, or confiscated by the government and are unlikely to be trafficked except through criminal kidnapping, a scourge that supplies an unknown number of children in the adoption market.

New Stricter Adoption Regulations: Reversing Reform

That the official crackdown on child trafficking is primarily a crackdown on de facto adoption was made clear by new stricter adoption regulations that were proposed in August 2011 as part of the effort to control child trafficking.[24]

As reported by *China Daily*, August 16, 2011, in the midst of a national antitrafficking campaign,

> The government is toughening rules to tackle the scourge of child trafficking, including making orphanages the only institutions that can offer abandoned children for adoption, an official said.
>
> "Illegal adoption," whereby adults can adopt without official registration, will also be targeted. . . .
>
> According to the revised rules, to be worked out jointly by the Ministry of Civil Affairs and CCCWA [China Center for Child Welfare and Adoption], all abandoned infants and young children should be sent to orphanages for adoption, Ji said.
>
> Once the new rules take effect, children adopted without the input of an orphanage will not be allowed to have a hukou, or household registration permit, Ji added.[25]

The new regulations reverse several previous, if sporadic, policy directions aimed at somewhat loosening adoption and registration restrictions in an effort to register more adoptions and restore rights to adopted and other hidden children, that is, to out-of-plan children. Specifically, in an effort to get more adoptions that take place outside of orphanages legally registered, the 1999 revisions to the adoption law facilitated the development of legal channels outside of orphanages to claim and register an adoption of an abandoned child or "legally relinquished child."[26] Various efforts to create a path for unregistered adopted children to get hukou have also been undertaken periodically since the late 1990s.[27] To be sure, these efforts have been limited and had limited success. However, the new adoption regulations seek to eliminate these external legal routes to adoption and to obtaining hukou, making all adoptions outside of orphanages illegal by requiring that all "abandoned" or relinquished children be put in an orphanage before being adopted. Children who are adopted outside of orphanages will be denied hukou by this official regulation of the central adoption authority of Civil Affairs.

There is at least some irony in the similarity between this outcome and the earlier efforts of state orphanages in Hunan to pull in abandoned children from other provinces, a practice that was eventually prosecuted as "child trafficking." Now central government policies, explicitly articulating this goal, use police busts to gather children from near and far and place them in state orphanages. Many of these children, found to have been "abandoned" or "sold" by birth parents rather than kidnapped, may be made available for official adoption, which in turn brings in hefty fees to the orphanages from adopters whether domestic or international. Under certain circumstances the illegal adopters may be permitted to keep the child, probably after paying these fees, if they have not obstructed the police "rescue" of the child and the birth parents are found to be the "seller," a crime for which they may be jailed.[28]

Above all, the current efforts to cut down on "child trafficking" are intended to make it even harder for adopted children to get hukou, reversing sporadic reform efforts to allow de facto adopted children to obtain a legal identity. Rather than relaxing the relinquishment, age and childless requirements in the adoption law in an effort to bring customary practices out into the open, and carrying out serious hukou reform to give every child born in China citizenship as a birthright regardless of whether they were born in accordance with birth planning regulations, the Ministry of Civil Affairs' plans to eliminate all domestic adoption outside of orphanages and deepen further its long-standing efforts to suppress customary adoption and deprive "illegal" children of hukou. Under the 1999 revisions to the adoption law, adoptions that occurred outside government channels could be considered legal and could be registered as long as the child was certified as "abandoned" by the police and the adopters were childless and over thirty, and followed certain registration procedures, including fees. This helped increase the numbers of registered adoptions in the early 2000s. Now these channels are to be narrowed or closed. That all of this is done in 2011 in the name of protecting child rights, rather than merely enforcing population control policies, is more than ironic.

The chance that these new regulations will succeed in eliminating de facto adoption is slim, although they will almost certainly lower the percentage of adoptions that are registered, turning some potentially legally registered adoptions into de facto illegal ones. These new regulations may also succeed in pulling more healthy children into orphanages again, a possibility that has not yet been investigated. After years of trying to suppress customary adoption practices and de facto adoptions, these adoptions still outnumber legal registered adoptions. Although the numbers of de facto adoptions are unknown, government officials in recent years estimate from small scale studies that they are more than four times the total number of domestic registered adoptions,[29] which in the 2000s hovered between 35,000 and 40,000 per year after briefly peaking at around 50,000 in 2000 in the wake of the 1999 legal revisions.[30] Registered adoptions have recently fallen below 25,000, with around 24,400 total adoptions registered in 2013, over 3,200 of which were international adoptions.[31] This falling number probably reflects the increased difficulty of registering adoptions that take place outside orphanages as well as the general decline in numbers of children available for adoption as we have already noted. One also expects that as adopters are increasingly stigmatized as "buyers," adopted children will increasingly be disguised as birth children, a strategy we saw in the past as a way to secure the child's status in the family and usually an easier route to get a hukou, although not even out-of-plan birth children are guaranteed a hukou today, especially in urban areas.[32]

Because the new adoption regulations actually reverse reform efforts to give hukou to unregistered adopted children, Civil Affairs' new approach may very well increase the numbers of unregistered children as an unintended consequence of this antitrafficking policy even though the numbers of out-of-plan children are falling. Unregistered children are, in turn, at greater risk of being undereducated, suffering from childhood diseases, being seized from either birth parents or adoptive parents, and, most ironically, being trafficked. These trends would promote the mirror opposite of the new global citizens that the Chinese government has hoped to create with its population policies and its efforts to rein in child trafficking.

Another possible immediate consequence is that the number of children who are confiscated from families and placed in orphanages, as seen in Gaoping and Zhenyuan, may increase. If these children then become part of an enlarged pool for official adoption, the Chinese government might be accused of engaging in the business of "manufacturing orphans" for the purpose of an official kind of child trafficking, as were the orphanages in Hunan that were prosecuted in 2005. As long as the government orphanages insist that adopters pay high mandatory donations, they too are "selling" children into adoption; some Chinese adopters today are willing to pay exorbitantly high "donation" fees to adopt a child from an orphanage, several times those charged for international adoption. The recent proposed regulations for centralizing and controlling all adoptions through orphanages put the government on a path headed in that direction and have already drawn criticism from some adopters, one of whom told us he felt his child had been treated like a commodity by the government orphanage.[33] However, the dominant and widely accepted discourse of the government's crackdown on child trafficking, which labels de facto adopters as "buyers," children as victims of kidnap, and the officials who confiscate children and place them in state orphanages as "rescuers," obscures the extent to which this pattern and the policies that underlie it resembles the government confiscation or "stealing" of children from families in Gaoping-Longhui and Zhenyuan for "ransom" or "sale" by state orphanages into adoption. The divergent discourses of "kidnap and ransom" (Gaoping and Zhenyuan) and "trafficking and rescue" cover more or less the same behavior.

Our research only touches on these complicated issues of child trafficking and government policy, although the patterns of relinquishment, adoption, and confiscation that we have found suggest important directions for new research and inquiry that reach beneath the surface of the current official and popular media discourse of child trafficking.

CHAPTER 6

*Conclusion: The Hidden Human
Costs of the One-Child Policy*

The Long Shadow of Loss: Personal Costs of Coerced Choices

The stories in this book demonstrate the long shadow cast by birth
planning policies on the lives of parents and their out-of-plan children who have struggled against these policies in various ways. The
long-term personal and interpersonal costs associated with adoption, abandonment, and the hiding of children are a notable feature
of the strategies and negotiations that birth families have made with
birth planning demands, beginning with the adopting out of an out-
of-plan child—generally a second or third daughter but sometimes
an overquota boy—for the purpose of avoiding punishments and
perhaps preserving a chance to try again for a needed son. When
the ability to openly adopt out a child to carefully chosen friends
and relatives—considered by local custom to be a responsible and
ethical arrangement for a child—was shut down by adoption regulations, making it necessary for people to turn to more secret and
extreme strategies of abandonment and hiding, the costs to those
involved escalated sharply. Parents we spoke to who felt compelled
to make the choice to permanently send away a child suffered for
many years from their loss, compounded by their own sense of

complicity in an act that violated normal parental responsibilities, risking their child's well-being no matter how carefully they tried to plan. Guilt and remorse are the consequences of "coerced choices" that led parents to do things they neither wanted to do nor felt were right. Children were also more likely to end up in the hands of sorely inadequate state institutions.

In our cases, some of the greatest human costs imposed by harsh birth planning policies emerge in the mid-2000s when strategies of hiding children became particularly risky in some areas, most notably areas where local birth planning officials had been put on notice to improve their record. The most gut-wrenching was the case of "Victory," an instance where local officials manufactured a "foundling" out of a hidden child whose parents struggled desperately to keep her, all in order to improve the officials' birth planning record and job ratings. The parents not only suffered the trauma of having their child literally ripped from their arms, but also a sense of guilt that they had failed utterly as parents to protect their child from this horrific act. They had failed to understand and anticipate the risks of hiding their born child, only knowing with certainty that to reveal her existence prior to her birth would result in her being aborted. In addition to the parents' suffering, the much-wanted daughter was forced to spend a year as an ostensibly "abandoned child" in a state institution and then was sent ten thousand miles away from her family and the community she was born into, creating a rupture that can never be repaired. Their case was not unique but echoed elsewhere in the country in the same time period, as other families, both adoptive and birth families, lost children they wanted to keep and raise.

While local Chinese adopters appear in many of these stories as welcome, if often serendipitous, beneficiaries of others' efforts to avoid birth planning restrictions and punishments, the stories from adopters, who are caught in the same population control system as birth parents, also reveal their costs and struggles to legalize a child's status and avoid losing the child to authorities after many years of raising the child "as if their own birth child." Some of these adoptive parents lost their children to authorities despite their best efforts to find a way to give their child a secure and legal status in their family. Over the last twenty years, unknown numbers of "unwanted," legally certified "abandoned children" in China's orphanages have been taken directly from the homes of would-be or existing adoptive families.

In our interviews, the impact of birth planning and the power of the government to deeply embed this policy is reflected in the indirectly-pressured or forced separation of parents and children, in the out-of-plan child's risks of losing multiple families during its childhood, in the out-of-plan child's loss of citizenship, basic entitlements, and even the right to grow up in its country of birth. Since the beginning of the 2000s, out-of-plan children have also increasingly faced the risks of being the objects of trafficking of various kinds.

Myths and the Uneven Terrain of International Adoption from China

Hopefully, this study also complicates the standard discourse, in the United States and in China, about why people jettisoned daughters from their families in the face of the one-child policy. The standard discourse asserts that the traditional patriarchal "son preference" of the Chinese family collided with the demands for population limitation to create female infant abandonment and other means of getting rid of unwanted girls so as to have another chance to produce a son. The stories and patterns documented here show a more complicated picture in which many Chinese families spontaneously welcomed and even sought out daughters in the face of punitive policies. Even families who continued to try for a son more often than not found ways to hold on to higher parity daughters through various ways of hiding them until after the birth of a boy, as parents of overquota boys, sometimes born in pursuit of a daughter, found ways to hide and eventually pay for their children. These families faced government-imposed impoverishment to do so.

These themes in turn lead to a reinterpretation of the larger discourse and critique of international adoption, including the way Chinese birth parents and Chinese adoptive parents are positioned as "others," if not made invisible, in this discourse. The rise of China as the world's largest supplier of children in international adoption proceeded under a set of hegemonic myths about Chinese culture and society. These myths asserted that due to an ancient cultural devotion to male bloodlines and a profound patriarchal devaluation of daughters, Chinese at the end of the twentieth century were reluctant to adopt children outside of their own bloodlines and they especially would not adopt the discarded daughters of strangers, the main burgeoning population in Chinese orphanages needing homes in the wake of the one-child policy. Even today in news stories about domestic adoption as "child trafficking," it is often asserted and echoed by foreign reporters that girls, being generally unwanted and unvalued, are trafficked for the dowries they can bring or as child brides, otherwise there is no way to explain why girls are even in the pool of children trafficked for adoption.[1]

As we have shown, these assertions are simply untrue; girls have been readily adopted as daughters throughout the era of the one-child policy. The counterhegemonic voices of both birth parents and adoptive parents, evident in the stories related here, complicate these simplistic, static notions of Chinese culture and society in important ways. Far from considering their girls to be "maggots in the rice" or "deeply unwanted, unvalued babies,"[2] sonless parents who gave up second or third daughters under duress in order to try to

have a son lived with regret and shame. Some went on to give birth
to and keep subsequent daughters, not ever wanting to repeat what
they had done.[3] Further, many of the "unwanted daughters" who
ended up in orphanages were in fact taken directly from adoptive
families who very much wanted to keep them but were not allowed
to do so. Some of the "unwanted daughters" were even seized directly from their own birth parents who found themselves helpless
in the face of local officials, who may have construed a hidden child
as an "illegal adoption." Under these conditions, the terrain of international adoption must be seen as built upon widespread coercion
as well as enormous inequality between those international parents
who have adopted the children who ended up in the government's
pool of "adoptable children" and those Chinese parents who lost
those children under conditions that made any sort of "voluntary
relinquishment" utterly impossible.

Thus, international adoption emerges as a product of harsh
state policies restricting births and suppressing the use of customary
adoption practices by ordinary villagers who wanted to incorporate
many of these children into their own families as daughters. In this
context, international adoption and the gains of relatively wealthy
North American and European adopters, including myself, must
be seen as having been obtained at great cost to others, being built
upon the losses of Chinese birth parents and Chinese adoptive families who under normal circumstances would have raised these children as part of their families. The implicit but very real competition
for allegedly "unwanted" Chinese children, clearly evident in recent
years,[4] has also been characterized by enormous inequality of power
and wealth, with the adoption of other people's children sanctioned
by two nation-states that premise this adoption on the child's "clean
break" with its previous family. The legal creation of a "clean break"
is demanded as much by US immigration policies governing the
issuance of immigrant visas and US citizenship to children adopted

from China by US citizens as by China's adoption policies.[5] Studies of international adoption and adoptee identity[6] suggest that this legal fiction is not in the interest of adoptees as they grow up and seek to shape an identity that makes sense of their place as a transnationally adopted person. Some of these adoptees want to find birth families and establish at least some kind of relationship in an effort to learn more about who they are and where they came from. As more adoptees from China search for their birth families, the "clean break" should give way to more open forms of adoption, as they have in US domestic adoptions, forms that do not so totally disadvantage and erase the birth family. Searching for origins will, above all, be severely hindered by the conditions in China that compelled birth parents to hide out-of-plan children through abandonment or through a local adoption that was disrupted by the government and then certified as an "abandonment." It will also be hindered by the extreme practices of some local officials who veritably kidnapped children from families and would, in retrospect, want to hide this.

In this international order and under the general rules of international adoption, endorsed by the Hague Convention on international adoption, those who have lost these children are not only powerless but also voiceless and unseen. Hopefully, this book will lessen their invisibility and provide the children who lost families in China with a better understanding of their origins in China, explaining how and why they were placed into an adoption outside of China, an understanding that goes beyond "the lowly value of daughters" and the traditional need for a son.

"Bare Life"—the Category of the Illegal Out-of-Plan Child

Looking through the lens of over three decades of child adoption, we see how birth planning has not merely infringed upon the reproductive choices of adults, but it has all too often abrogated the basic rights and needs of out-of-plan children, a category of children who are without a legal existence.[7] This is a group of children, both boys and girls, whose life chances are hampered in various ways compared to "planned" children. At the most basic level, out-of-plan children's rights to their family are called into question and put at risk, in addition to suffering disadvantages in education and basic health care compared to peers due to lack of legal registration.[8]

As China entered the twenty-first century as a rising international power, increasingly confident of its place in a modern global order, millions of mostly rural children born out of plan have been implicitly if not explicitly acceptable collateral damage of population control policies; the families responsible for them have been punished and intentionally impoverished; parent-to-child ethical obligations have been distorted and violated, and normal people have felt pressured or compelled to do things that they themselves felt were wrong, becoming actively complicit in the losses imposed upon them and their children by state policy. Other parents, albeit fewer in number, have been made fully powerless to hold on to their children in the face of authorities who take out-of-plan children away from families in order to meet a population quota. In short, the rights and well-being of out-of-plan children have been implicitly, and sometimes explicitly, accepted as the necessary collateral damage of the over three-decade long birth planning project. This is the underbelly of the processes that have created China's new "global citizens," a generation of increasingly well-educated, planned children, often raised as an only child in child-centered urban families.[9] The stark inequalities in opportunity and status created by these policies can only be addressed when the policies, once and for all, are abolished.

The kinds of changes to the one-child policy that have been recently touted as a loosening the policy, such as allowing a couple in which one is a singleton (only child) to have two children, effectively expand the existing categories of exceptions such as the rural 1.5-child policy and the rule that two married singletons can have two children, both policy exceptions that go back to the 1980s. But the expansion of exceptions does not fundamentally change a policy that is enforced by punishing those who give birth outside the approved categories or specified timing, thus leaving in place the deeply embedded apparatus that enforces and benefits from this policy.[10] This in turn perpetuates a process that will continue to recruit children into the category of "out-of-plan" child, even if in smaller numbers than in the past. The out-of-plan child continues to be born with an exorbitant price on its head, a price that someone must pay, and is deprived of hukou, the sine qua non of citizenship, as a means of punishing its parents. This in turn encourages parents to hide children and officials to deny their rights even when they know of their existence, creating the panoply of vulnerabilities for the child that have been shown here—being relinquished, abandoned, seized from a home, put in an institution, trafficked, sent out of the country—depriving these children of the secure attachments to family and community that young children should have.

In essence, "voluntary relinquishment" by any reasonable definition and as demanded by The Hague Convention and any ethical international adoption program was nearly impossible under the conditions that prevailed in China in this era. Whether referring to the waves of outright abandonment of the 1990s or the direct seizure of "illegal" children by officials reported in the 2000s (which also occurred earlier), "it was all coercion," as one Chinese adoptee put it after a talk at an adoption reunion in England recently. Relinquishment was almost always coerced in one way or another.

The law itself made relinquishment illegal except under very extreme conditions, virtually insuring that more parents would turn to abandonment in the face of birth planning assaults. Then, in almost catch-22 fashion, the act of abandonment was considered tantamount to voluntary relinquishment and obviated the ethical need for "informed consent" in the adoption process. As overt abandonment has declined the continued threat of impoverishing fines coupled with the lack of legal channels to relinquish children pressures some poor parents to turn to middle men and traffickers to hide unauthorized birth.

Furthermore, the problems discussed here—abandoned children forced to endure months if not years living in inadequate institutions, children losing multiple families that wanted them, children being shuffled from place to place to hide them, children deprived of citizenship and legal identities, as well as the pain suffered by millions of parents—all arise from the regulations and laws promulgated by the state and implemented through the administrative apparatus of the government, with enforcement from top to bottom insured by a set of administrative measures designed to reward local success and punish local failure to enforce policies and meet targets. It is not primarily the corruption or abuse of these laws by the local officials who enforce them but the enforcement of these laws and policies governing births and adoptions that has created the lion's share of the problems and suffering of parents and children discussed here.

Expanding categories of exception to the rules of the one-child policy does not change these liabilities for those children who are born outside of those categories, some of whom will struggle their entire lives from their lack of status.[11] The recent change to a two-child rule, which will replace the urban one-child rule and rural one-son-or-two-child rule, is an improvement that will reduce further the number of children born out of plan and may well reduce reported sex ratios at birth. However, only an end to this policy can abolish the category of out-of-plan child and end the widespread practice of making certain children collateral damage in a war against population growth, now waged in the name of lessening environmental destruction and mitigating global warming.

Disentangling common adoption practices from child trafficking and child abuse also requires an end to the policies that create unregistered, at-risk children in the first place, the very policies that have created the category of the illegal "out-of-plan" child.[12] Depriving de facto adopted children of access to the rights of citizenship as articulated in current adoption policies, further deepening policies that have long been tied to birth planning needs rather than child welfare needs, will do little to stop trafficking but will almost certainly increase the numbers of unregistered children who are vulnerable and at risk. That a policy of withholding a child's citizenship is now rationalized as a measure against child trafficking, in addition to providing support to birth planning policies, makes it no less a violation of the child's rights. One can only hope that after more than thirty years, with a national total fertility rate well below replacement level in the last two censuses, the policy that has marked this era and scarred so many children and punished so many parents might finally come to an end, taking its place in the proverbial trash bin of history alongside other practices that, in retrospect, we can see as the atrocities that they always were.

ACKNOWLEDGMENTS

In addition to Huang Banghan and Wang Liyao, my primary Chinese collaborators whom I thanked in the preface of this book, I would like to thank my friends and colleagues in the China adoption community who inspired and helped me to complete this book, a task that became more difficult after the death of my co-researcher and old friend Wang Liyao, whose capacity for empathy has guided me in telling the stories contained here. In the wake of this loss, Hanni Beyer, a friend of Lao Wang's, generously took time to read a rough draft when I needed the perspective and support of a fellow adoptive parent. Over the years, Families with Children from China (FCC) and, more recently, Children Adopted from China (CACH–Great Britain) have provided an audience for my scholarly work and a shared commitment to learning about our children's origins in China. I owe special thanks to Amy Klatzkin and my previous publisher Brian Boyd who helped me reach this audience ten years ago by editing and publishing *Wanting a Daughter, Needing a Son*, the prequel to this book.

For over twenty years I was fortunate to have the opportunity to coteach with Betsy Hartmann, professor of Development Studies and director of the Population and Development Program at

Hampshire College, and to learn from her in the classroom. Her engaged scholarship and activism on behalf of reproductive rights globally and in the United States has been an inspiration for my work. I am also grateful to my former teacher and mentor Edward Friedman, who continues to offer wise counsel to his many former students. He kindly read my manuscript in its final stages, encouraging me at last to publish it. Thanks are owed to my editor at the University of Chicago Press, John Tryneski, who had edited my first academic book over thirty years ago. He patiently represented, and at times defended, my authorial views at the press and helped me bring this final product to fruition.

My spouse and coparent Bill Grohmann has provided logistical, editorial, and emotional support for more than twenty years of research, taking care of our now-grown children, our home, and our many pets during my long trips to China. He read numerous drafts of this book, always providing sound advice and encouragement.

Above all, I would like to thank my daughter LiLi from whom I have learned so much about being on the other side of international adoption, first when she was a thoughful and perceptive child and now as a critical young scholar in American studies, able to articulate what it means to be an American transracial adoptee from China.

NOTES

PREFACE

1. That experience is recounted in Kay Johnson, "Chinese Orphanages: Saving China's Abandoned Girls," *Australian Journal of Chinese Affairs*, no. 30 (July 1993): 67–84.

2. Tyrene White, *China's Longest Campaign: Birth Planning in the People's Republic, 1949–2005* (Ithaca, NY: Cornell University Press, 2006), chap. 8, especially 225–28.

3. Mei-ling Hopgood, *Lucky Girl: A Memoir* (Chapel Hill, NC: Alonquin Books, 2009), 30–31.

4. This quote is from Kate Blewett in *The Dying Rooms*, directors Brian Wood and Kate Blewett, Lauderdale Productions, 1995.

5. *The Dying Rooms*, 1995; Robin Munroe and Jeff Rigsby, *Death by Default: A Policy of Fatal Neglect in China's State Orphanages* (New York: Human Rights Watch, 1996).

CHAPTER ONE

1. Laura Briggs, *Somebody's Children: The Politics of Transnational Adoption* (Durham, NC: Duke University Press, 2012), 18. Briggs cites Elizabeth Bartholet in particular, the author of an influential book, *Family Bonds: Adoption and the Politics of Parenting* (New York: Houghton Mifflin, 1993) and more recently *Nobody's Children* (Boston: Beacon Press, 2000) about the US foster care system.

2. Only recently have the voices of Chinese adoptees emerged as those adopted in the 1990s become young adults. E.g., see *Somewhere Between*, produced by Linda Goldstein Knowlton (Docuramafilms, 2012).

3. An exception is the *Invisible Red Thread*, produced by Maureen Marovich, directed by Changfu Chang and Marovich (Picture This Films, 2011), which includes a Chinese adoptive family of a teenage girl living in Jiangxi. Other films by Changfu Chang prominently feature birth parents but also include adoptive parents. See Chang, *Sophia's Story and also Daughters' Return*

4. Tyrene White, "Domination, Resistance, and Accommodation in China's One-Child Campaign," in *Chinese Society: Change, Conflict, and Resistance*, ed. Perry and Selden, 171–96, 3rd ed. (New York: Routledge, 2010).

5. Ethan Michelson, "Family Planning Enforcement in Rural China: Enduring State-Society Conflict," in *Growing Pains: Tensions and Opportunity in China's Transformation* ed. Jean Oi, Scott Rozelle, and Xueguang Zhou, chap. 8.(Stanford, CA: Walter Shorenstein Asia Pacific Research Center, 2010), 193.

6. For a brief sketch of the rise and decline of international adoption from China, see Kay Johnson, "Adoption in China," in *Encyclopedia of Modern China* (New York: Charles Scribner's Sons, 2009).

7. See Kay Johnson, "Saving China's Abandoned Girls," *Australian Journal of Chinese Affairs*, no. 30 (July 1993): 67–84, and Kay Johnson, "Politics of International and Domestic Adoption in China," *Law and Society Review* 36, no. 2 (2002): 379–96.

8. In this book, I identify our main research area as rural "central China" or "south central China." It is an area that is also sometimes included as part of "east China." The research took place mostly in one province but included bordering provinces and a few more distant areas. I do not identify the research area more precisely in order to obscure identities.

9. Kay Ann Johnson, *Wanting a Daughter, Needing a Son: Abandonment, Adoption, and Orphanage Care in China*, ed. Amy Klatzkin (Minneapolis: Yeong and Yeong, 2004).

10. In Chinese, the terms "out of plan" (*jiwai*) and "overquota" (*chaosheng*) are sometimes used interchangeably. Overquota implies that the number of births has exceeded those allowed by the rules. Out of plan is a broader category that includes children who are born outside marriage or to parents below the legal marriage age, children born before the required interval between births, or children whose birth has been hidden by parents, regardless of timing or birth number, and are therefore not registered. Such unauthorized children lack a

legal existence or identity unless and until they are registered, something that may be prohibited under local regulations or practice even after fines and punishment have been meted out. As we will see, the registered identities of unauthorized children may also be false, making their legality dubious if discovered.

11. Shuzhuo Li, Yexia Zhang, and Marcus Feldman, "Birth Registration in China: Problems, Practices, and Policies," *Population Research and Policy Review* 29 (2010): 297–317, doi:10.1007/s11113-009-9141-x, http://www.springerlink .com.proxy2.hampshire.edu/content/p062746721026124/fulltext.pdf.

12. See, e.g., Weixing Zhu, Li Lu, and Terese Hesketh, "China's Excess Males, Sex Selective Abortion, and the One Child Policy: Analysis of Data from the 2005 National Intercensus Survey," *British Medical Journal*, April 9, 2009 (BMJ. 2009; 338: b1211), http://www.ncbi.nlm.nih.gov/pmc/articles /PMC2667570/; Valerie Hudson and Andrea M. den Boer, *Bare Branches: The Security Implications of Asia's Excess Male Population* (Cambridge, MA: MIT Press, 2004); Feng Wang, "China's Population Destiny: The Looming Crisis," Brookings Research, September 2010, http://www.brookings.edu /research/articles/2010/09/china-population-wang.

13. http://www.64tianwang.com/bencandy.php?fid-7-id-10243-page-1.htm. A similar case in Xiamen in October 2010 also received wide publicity in the news and Chinese Internet: "Forced Abortions for Chinese Women," Al Jazeera, October 20, 2010, http://www.aljazeera.com/news/asia-pacific/2010 /10/201010208145793266.html.

14. Susan Greenhalgh remarked upon the largely unrecorded human costs of "China's grand experiment in state birth planning," although it was in human terms a "colossal tragedy." Susan Greenhalgh and Edwin Winckler, *Governing China's Population* (Stanford, CA: Stanford University Press, 2005), 319.

15. Kay Johnson, "Challenging the Discourse of Intercountry Adoption: Perspectives from Rural China," in *Intercountry Adoption*, ed. Judith Gibbons and Karen Rotabi, 103–17 (Burlington, VT: Ashgate, 2012).

16. Zhang Longxi, *Mighty Opposites: From Dichotomies to Differences in the Comparative Study of China* (Stanford, CA: Stanford University Press, 1998).

17. Author's personal communications. I also contributed an op-ed piece to the *Boston Globe* on this film and a Human Rights in Asia book, *Death by Default*, that followed quickly on its heels. "Sorrow of the Orphans," *Boston Globe Sunday Globe, Focus*, February 11, 1996.

18. Interviews and discussions with adoptive parents.

19. Bruce Porter, "I Met My Daughter at the Wuhan Foundling Hospital . . . Un-

wanted and Abandoned, Baby Girls Have Become the Newest Chinese Export," *New York Times Magazine*, April 11, 1993. Also see Elaine Louis, "Now Chosen, Chinese Girls Take to the US," *New York Times*, April 27, 1995.

20. Ellen Goodman, "Cloe's First Fourth," *Boston Globe*, July 3, 2003, A13.

21. Mathew Guterl, in *Seeing Race in Modern America* (Chapel Hill, NC: University of North Carolina, 2013), argues that multiracial adoptive families are visually projected as a politically progressive global ideal that shows the "triumph of enlightened reason over irrational prejudice," pointing out that "one hundred years ago, such co-mingled families were unthinkable" (85–86).

22. Grazi Poso Christie, "Choose Adoption, Not Abortion," *USA Today*, January 14, 2014, http://www.usatoday.com/story/opinion/2014/01/18/march-life-abortion-roe-wade-column/4523723/.

23. Barbara Yngvesson, *Belonging in an Adopted World: Race, Identity, and Transnational Adoption* (Chicago: University of Chicago Press, 2010).

24. Xinran, *Message from an Unknown Chinese Mother: Stories of Loss and Love* (New York: Scribner, 2010). According to Joshua Zhang, the director of CCAI, a large adoption agency specializing in China adoption, in contrast to the United States, "The concept (of adoption) hardly exists in Chinese society. Nobody knows about it." Vivien Chiu, "From China with Love," *South China Morning Post*, August 15, 1999. Adoption agency directors that I spoke with in the 1990s routinely repeated to clients a belief that Chinese do not adopt and especially will not adopt girls.

25. Statistics on registered adoptions from Minzheng tongji nianjian 1999–2010; interviews with Civil Affairs officials, 1996.

26. One such locally adopted girl is featured meeting a same-age Canadian adopted teen from the same area in Marovich and Changfu Chang, *Invisible Red Thread*.

27. Peter Selman, personal communication, based on calculations from statistics reported to The Hague.

28. E.g., see *The Invisible Red Thread*.

29. James Lee and Wang Feng, in *One-Quarter of Humanity: Malthusian Mythology and Chinese Reality* (Cambridge, MA: Harvard University Press, 1999), 8–9, argue that frequent adoption was a distinctive feature of Chinese kinship compared to Europe. Nor is adoption necessarily more stigmatized in China than in the United States; in both countries biological ties are constructed as normative and more valued as the basis for family and kinship. See Nicholas

Park and Patricia Hill, "Is Adoption an Option?," *Journal of Family Issues* 35, no. 5 (April 2014): 601–26, http://jfi.sagepub.com/content/35/5/601.

30. The term "one-child policy" is used generically in this book, as in most official Chinese publications, to refer to the 1979 policy and the variations that emerged in most rural areas in the 1980s. When referring specifically to the variations, they will be specified; the most notable is a one-son-two-child policy, sometimes known as a 1.5-child policy, whereby a second birth is allowed several years after the birth of a girl. The 1.5-child policy became prevalent in most nonminority rural areas by the late 1980s; minority areas usually are allowed two spaced children, sometimes more. Until recently the only exception allowed in urban areas was that two singletons (the only child in their family) could have two spaced children. In 2014 it was announced that a couple with one singleton spouse may be allowed two children.

31. In our earlier research, almost 80 percent of nearly eight hundred adoption cases involved girls, about 60 percent of whom were foundlings. See Johnson, *Wanting a Daughter, Needing a Son*, 102–5. This finding is also confirmed by Weiguo Zhang, "Who Adopts Girls and Why?," *China Journal*, no. 56 (July 2006). Much of his research comes from a rural area on the North China plain, indicating that our findings are not confined to the central south region and areas around the Yangzi that we studied.

32. "China Baby Trafficking: 1,094 Suspects Arrested," Sky News, February 28, 2014.

33. Amy Kasmin, Patti Waldmeir and Kirija Shuvakumar suggest that the practice is still widespread in "Asia: Heirs and Spares," *Financial Times*, July 10, 2011, http://www.ft.com/intl/cms/s/0/54751678-ab1a-11e0-b4d8-00144feabdc0.html#axzz1V1igqs22. Evidence is based partly on an interview with a twenty-eight-year-old "child bride" from Fujian. Reporter Liao Huijian interviews a thirty-five-year-old child bride from Fujian in "Child Brides Resurface in China with Shortage of Females," *Want China Times*, May 30, 2011, http://www.wantchinatimes.com/news-subclass-cnt.aspx?cid=1503&MainCatID=&id=20110530000003. This and other evidence suggests that the custom of adopting a girl as a "future daughter in law" was briefly revived in the 1980s in Fujian where it had been particularly widespread in the past. We found only two cases in our sample (both from before 1990) from central south China where the custom was never widespread.

34. Avraham Ebenstein, "The Missing Girls of China and the Unintended Conse-

quences of the One Child Policy," *Journal of Human Resources* 45, no. 1 (Winter 2010): 9.

35. This fits an earlier finding of Greenhalgh, from fieldwork in another part of China, about the perceived burden of more than one son that emerged in the 1980s and an increasing value placed on having a daughter. See for, e.g., Susan Greenhalgh, Zhu Chuzhu, and Li Nan, "Restraining Population Growth in Three Chinese Villages, 1988–1993," *Population and Development Review* 20, no. 2 (1994): 365–95.

36. Mo Yan, *Frog*, trans. Howard Greenblatt (New York: Penguin Press, 2015); Ma Jian, *The Dark Road*, trans. Flora Drew (New York: Penguin Press, 2013). Also see Xinran, *Message from an Unknown Chinese Mother*.

37. This material is discussed in depth in chapter 4 of Johnson, *Wanting a Daughter, Needing a Son.*

38. Laurel Bossen, "Forty Million Missing Girls," ZNet, October 7, 2005, http://www.zcommunications.org/forty-million-missing-girls-by-laurel-bossen.

39. Weiguo Zhang, in contrast to Bossen above, also finds this increasingly positive attitude toward daughters evolving in rural areas of Hebei in the 1990s in response to economic and structural changes associated with post-Mao rural reforms. "Is a Married-Out Daughter Like Spilt Water?," *Modern China* 35, no. 3 (May 2009): 256–83 Yongxiang Yan, "Girl Power: Young Girls and the Waning of Patriarch in Rural North China," *Ethnology* 45, no. 2 (Spring 2006): 105–23, http://www.jstor.org/stable/4617569.

40. Daniel Goodkind, "Child Underreporting, Fertility, and Sex Ratio Imbalance in China," *Demography* 48 (2011): 291–316, doi:10.1007/s13524-010-0007-y provides an interesting analysis that helps explain how "daughter preference" might occur in, even contribute to, areas with the highest reported sex ratios.

41. This is a major finding of Weiguo Zhang as well, "Who Adopts Girls and Why?," *China Journal* 56 (July 2006): 2–19. Interestingly US adoption agencies and research indicate that the preference for daughters among international adopters is very strong, reflecting perhaps the cultural construction of girls as more adoptable than boys and better suited to adoption, where parent-child ties are based on caring relationships rather than biological ties. Also see Zhang, "Is a Married-Out Daughter Like Spilt Water?" A study by Liu et al. that looks at earlier patterns of adoption through census materials also finds a two-gender ideal reflected in adoption patterns from the 1950s to 1980s. See Liu Jihong et al., "Factors Affecting Adoption in China, 1950–1980," *Population Studies* 58, no. 1 (March 2004): 21–36.

42. Greenhalgh et al. found changes in attitudes toward daughters in her early research in Shaanxi in the 1980s/early 1990s. See "Restraining Population Growth." Also see *Governing China's Population*, 283–84. Also see Hong Zhang, "Bracing for an Uncertain Future: A Case Study of New Coping Strategies of Rural Parents under China's Birth Control Policy," *China Journal* 54 (July 2005): 53–76.

43. Vanessa Fong, *Only Hope: Coming of Age under China's One Child Policy* (Stanford, CA: Stanford University Press, 2004).

44. Personal communication with Ralph Thaxton about his extensive research in rural Henan.

45. See Johnson, *Wanting a Daughter, Needing a Son*, 85, for an analysis of 205 abandonment cases.

46. From unpublished research. About 70 percent of approximately eight hundred unregistered children in our sample were living with or being temporarily hidden by birth parents; around 30 percent of hidden children were children living permanently in adoptive families, most of them foundlings.

47. Greenhalgh and Winckler, *Governing China's Population*, comments on the cultural cost of ethical anxieties created by consequences such as skewed sex ratios and the treatment of girls (265) and moral costs (247–48). In our research we see some of the individual personal costs of these ethical breaches.

48. The term "coercion" is used here broadly to include all penalties intended to punish out-of-plan births, ranging from financial penalties, loss of property, job loss or demotion, mandated or pressured sterilization and abortion, to taking a child, sometimes with the use of force. More recent terminology that calls a birth planning fine a "social compensation fee" does not alter the fact this is intended as punishment and is way outside the range and purpose of a normal government tax mandate. In any setting outside of China, all of these methods of inducing compliance with birth planning rules would be considered highly "coercive."

49. Pang Jiaoming, *The Orphans of Shao: A True Account of the Blood and Tears of the One-child Policy in China* (New York: Women's Rights in China Publishers, 2014), 200 (English version).

50. Even in urban settings, people may still be subject to overt, even violent coercion, such as a widely publicized case in Xiamen just before the census in 2010 (in note 13), "Forced Abortions for Chinese Women," Al Jazeera, October 20, 2010. Perhaps not coincidentally, this case involved a woman with a nonurban household registration (hukou).

51. For, e.g., Sara Dorow and Amy Swiffen, "Blood and Desire: The Secret of Heteronormativity in Adoption Narratives of Culture," *American Ethnologist* 36, no. 3 (August 2009): 563–73. Also see Heather Jacobson, *Culture Keeping: White Mothers, International Adoption, and the Negotiation of Family Difference* (Nashville, TN: Vanderbilt University Press, 2008).

52. Most scholars of population policy describe an evolution toward less coercive methods beginning in the mid-1990s. See, e.g., Greenhalgh and Winckler, *Governing China's Population*, chap. 5; Tyrene White, *China's Longest Campaign: Birth Planning in the People's Republic, 1949–2005* (Ithaca, NY: Cornell University Press, 2006), chap. 9.

53. Typically, Karin Evans, in her account of adopting a girl from China and why girls are abandoned, quotes a famous third-century Chinese poet: "How sad it is to be a woman! Nothing on earth is held so cheap." *The Lost Daughters of China* (New York: Tarcher, 2000), 30.

54. E.g., Laura Briggs, "Making 'American' Families: Transnational Adoption and US Latin America Policy," in *Haunted by Empire*, ed. Ann Stoler, 344–65 (Durham, NC: Duke University Press, 2006).

55. E.g., E. J. Graff, "The Lie We Love," *Foreign Policy*, November 1, 2008.

56. The convention states that international adoption should be used only when domestic adoption is not possible.

57. Convention on the Protection of Children and Co-operation in Respect of Intercountry Adoption, May 29, 1993, www.hcch.net/upload/conventions/txt33en.pdf.

58. Demographer Yong Cai calculated the figure is no more than 100 million, one-fourth the oft-repeated governmental claim. Hvinstendahl, "Has China Outgrown the One Child Policy?," *Science* 329, no. 5998 (September 17, 2010): 1458–61, doi:10.1126/science.329.5998.1458. Also see Martin Whyte, Wang Feng, and Yong Cai, "Challenging Myths about China's One-Child Policy," *China Journal*, no. 74 (July 2015), pp. 144-159, and Susan Greenhalgh, *Cultivating Global Citizens: Population in the Rise of China* (Cambridge, MA: Harvard University Press, 2010), 121.

59. Betsy Hartmann, "The Great Distraction: 'Overpopulation' Is Back in Town," CommonDreams.org, August 30, 2011, http://www.BetsyHartmann.com and http://popdev.hampshire.edu.

60. "China Child Fines 'Spark Riot,'" BBC News, May 21, 2007, http://news.bbc.co.uk/2/hi/asia-pacific/6677273.stm; also the case of Chen Guangcheng, the "blind activist" who took local officials to court for birth planning abuses and

recent cases of forced late abortions surface to show the continuing problems of coercion that are inextricably embedded in the system.

CHAPTER TWO

1. As suggested earlier, in this book I will often use the term "relinquishment" as a generic term that encompasses a wide range of arrangements that remove a child from its family, ranging from openly arranging an adoption or directly handing a child over to other caregivers to anonymously leaving a child unattended in a private or public place. The term "relinquishment" is not used to denote the degree of voluntariness or duress in giving up a child. Some "relinquished" children have been forcefully seized from parents; indeed all relinquishments here may be seen as coerced in some way. Furthermore, it is often difficult to distinguish the difference between various forms of relinquishment, such as adopting-out and "abandoning" a child on a carefully chosen doorstep, although sometimes this is clear. The cases presented will illustrate the range of possibilities.

2. Pseudonyms are used throughout this book; most specific place names are avoided.

3. Interview with Huang Mei in her home, 2004.

4. The growing importance of daughters in the family has been noted by others. E.g., Weiguo Zhang, "Is a Married-Out Daughter Like Spilt Water?," *Modern China* 35, no. 3 (May 2009): 256–83; Yan Yunxiang, "Girl Power: Young Women and the Waning of Patriarchy in North China," *Ethnology* 45, no. 2 (Spring 2006): 105–23; Greenhalgh and Winckler, *Governing China's Population*, 283–84. We heard much anecdotal confirmation of this, including the importance of adopted daughters.

5. Weiguo Zhang finds that daughters were increasingly able to provide support for parents after marriage under the economic reforms initiated in the 1980s. Zhang, "Is a Married-Out Daughter Like Spilt Water?"

6. Interviewed in her home, 2004.

7. Interview in her village home, 2004.

8. Interviews in her home, 1996, 2009, March and July 2010.

CHAPTER THREE

1. Sten Johansson and Ola Nygren, "The Missing Girls of China: A New Demographic Account," *Population and Development Review* 17, no. 1 (1991): 35–51.

2. These findings are discussed in greater detail in chapter 4 of Johnson, *Wanting a Daughter, Needing a Son*.

3. After 2005, the numbers of international adoption declined quickly from four-
    teen thousand to below four thousand after 2010. The composition of the chil-
    dren adopted also changed quickly from primarily healthy infants to well over
    half being disabled and significantly older, including more boys. Peter Selman,
    "The Global Decline in International Adoption: What Lies Ahead?," *Social
    Policy and Society* 11, no. 3 (July 2012): 381–97.

4. Over four hundred thousand if Johansson's estimates from the late 1980s are
    any indication for this period. Sten Johansson and Ola Nygren, "The Missing
    Girls of China: A New Demographic Account," *Population and Development
    Review* 17 (March 1991): 35–51.

5. An important exception is the work of Weiguo Zhang.

6. Interview, 1996; multiple follow-up interviews, 1998–2010.

7. The practice of *tongyangxi*, or adopting baby girls as "foster daughters-in-law"
    to become future brides of sons, was known to be very common in parts of
    the southeast and Taiwan, although we were told it was not very common in
    this area and was rare after the 1950s. Arthur Wolf, "Adopt a Daughter-in-Law,
    Marry a Sister: A Chinese Solution to the Problem of the Incest Taboo," *Amer-
    ican Anthropologist* 70 (1968): 866–74.

8. Studies of *tongyangxi* in other areas and time periods have found that the re-
    sulting marital relationships had lower fertility than other kinds of marriages,
    speculatively due to the culturally strained nature of such a marital relationship
    whereby children raised as siblings are married. Perhaps this was the case with
    Wu Dazhu and his wife. Ibid.

9. Interview, in a town near their home, 2004.

10. Interview, 2009.

11. Valerie M. Hudson and Andrea M. Den Boer, *Bare Branches: The Security
    Implications of Asia's Surplus Male Population* (Cambridge, MA: MIT Press,
    2004); Mara Hvistendahl, *Unnatural Selection* (New York: Public Affairs,
    2011).

12. For an excellent critique of the dominant discourse about the social dangers
    presented by bachelors, a discourse that resonates with the official Chinese dis-
    course, see Susan Greenhalgh, "Patriarchal Demographics? China's Sex Ratio
    Reconsidered," *Population and Development Review* 38, supplement (2012):
    130–49.

13. Interviews in his home, 2009, 2010, 2011.

14. Susan Greenhalgh, "Patriarchal Demographics?," points out that the official,

scholarly, and popular discourse on the rising bachelor population casts them as "not quite human."

15. Interviews, 2009, 2010.

16. The information on hidden or "black children" discussed here is drawn from questionnaires given to over eight hundred households between 2000 and 2005 who had unregistered children and from formal and informal interviews over the years of this research, 1996–2015.

17. Interviews, 1999, 2000.

18. Interviews, 2008, 2009, 2010.

19. The story of this seizure is told in chapter 4 below.

20. Weiguo Zhang, "Is a Married-Out Daughter Like Spilt Water?"

21. Ethan Michelson, "Family Planning Enforcement in Rural China: Enduring State-Society Conflict?," in *Growing Pains: Tensions and Opportunity in China's Transformation*, ed. Jean Oi, Scott Rozelle, and Xueguang Zhou (Stanford, CA: Walter Shorenstein Asia-Pacific Research Center, 2009), chap. 8. Noncompliance with birth planning birth quotas in the countryside was estimated to be about 30 percent of births in the mid-1990s.

22. Correspondence, 2002.

23. Interviews, 2009, 2010.

24. The two girls, born less than a year apart, were born using one birth permission certificate; one of the girls needed to be hidden so the mother could get permission for another birth. Two more girls were born and secretly adopted out before the son was finally born.

25. Interview, 2000.

26. A case of a twenty-year-old unregistered girl, a "black child" fighting for the right to a hukou in Beijing, was recently recounted in "Fighting for Identity," *Economist*, May 17, 2014. Several current cases are also reported in Nathan VanderKlippe, "The Ghost Children: In the Wake of China's One-Child Policy, a Generation Is Lost," *Globe and Mail*, March 13, 2015, http://www .theglobeandmail.com/news/world/the-ghost-children-in-the-wake-of -chinas-one-child-policy-a-generation-is-lost/article23454402/. Officials estimate 13 million people fall into this category, but this is at best an educated guess from census data and is probably too low.

27. Our research, like Johansson, found that the percentage of adopted boys diminishes in the 1990s, although it remains a significant portion, around 20 percent of our adoptive family sample that consists primarily of adoptions that

occurred from the late 1980s onward. It appears that nearly all healthy relinquished boys, like many healthy girls, were adopted by the local population without ever reaching government hands.

28. The struggle for a hukou in urban areas is particularly difficult as many adoptive parents I met told me. A group of adoptive parents I first met in Beijing in the late 1990s fought unsuccessfully for over a decade to obtain hukou for their adopted "found" children, forming an officially persecuted, now-defunct group called "The Sunflower." The single woman who organized this group came under such heavy pressure from family and officials she suffered an emotional breakdown, resulting in her seven-year-old adopted daughter being taken to the Beijing orphanage.

29. Shuzhuo Li, Yexia Zhang, and Marcus W. Feldman, "Birth Registration in China: Practices, Problems and Policies," *Population Research Policy Review* 29 (2010): 297–317, doi:10.1007/s11113-009-9141-x.

30. Jihong Liu, Grace Wyshak, and Ulla Larsen, "Physical Well-Being and School Enrolment: A Comparison of Adopted and Biological Children in One-Child Families," *Social Science & Medicine* 59 (2004): 609–23, doi:10.1016/j.socscimed.2003.11.008.

31. This information is taken from a Hefei news story in *Hefei Evening News*, "*Found 'Black Child' Still Has Not Obtained a Hukou*," *Hefei Wanbao*, February 2, 2010, and author's follow-up interview with the father, June 2010.

CHAPTER FOUR

1. Paul Goodman, "Stealing Babies for Adoption," *Washington Post*, March 12, 2006, A01.

2. Barbara Demick, "Some Chinese Parents Say Their Children Were Stolen for Adoption," *Los Angeles Times*, September 20, 2009, http://articles.latimes.com/2009/sep/20/world/fg-china-adopt20.

3. Kate Blewett and Brian Woods, producers, *China's Stolen Children*, directed by Jezza Neuman (True Vision Productions, 2008).

4. Interviews with orphanage officials (Hefei, Feixi, Fuyang, Wuhan), 2000–2011. Interviews with adoption facilitators, 2011.

5. Although these legal changes were not implemented everywhere, registered domestic adoptions from orphanages and outside of orphanages increased from less than ten thousand per year in the 1990s to a high of fifty thousand in 2000, remaining slightly below this level before falling again at the end of the

decade. These figures come from the annual volumes of the *China Civil Affairs Statistical Yearbook* (Zhongguo Minzheng tongji nianjian).

6. Interviews, 2001.

7. We found that in many places this gap in fees closed as the 2000s progressed and soon disappeared as Chinese incomes grew and fees paid by all adopters evened out. Because domestic adoption fees were not centrally regulated as international fees were, wealthy domestic adopters might even pay more in some instances.

8. "Welfare Institutes' Income Paid by Foreign Adoption Donations Questioned," *Beijing News*, June 9, 2011, http://blog.sina.com.cn/s/blog_4ab34fd101017ko3 .htm (Chinese). Caixin pointedly headlined their stories about Shaoyang "baby selling": Shangguan Jiaoming, "In Hunan, Family Planning Turns to Plunder," CaixinOnline, May 10, 2011, http://english.caixin.com/2011-05-10 /100257756.html?p0#page1.

9. Prospective adopters turned to the Internet, various kinds of middlemen, and networks that supplied children, fueling criminal child trafficking. This will be discussed later in this chapter.

10. Demographic evidence suggests that over all fertility declined to nearly current levels by the mid-1990s; however, in our interviews the expressed fertility desires in rural areas were noticeably lower in 2010 than when we started this research in 1995.

11. E.g., see Hannah Beech, "China's Baby Traffickers," *Time*, January 8, 2001, http://www.time.com/time/asia/magazine/2001/0108/babies.smuggle .html; "Court Convicts 52 of Baby-Trafficking in China," *New York Times*, July 7, 2004, http://www.nytimes.com/2004/07/24/world/court-convicts -52-of-baby-trafficking-in-china.html.

12. In several interviews in 2009, rural women told us they intended to stop at one daughter even though allowed another birth. Our findings mirrored the more extensive findings of Hong Zhang in rural Hubei in the same time period. Hong Zhang, "From Resisting to 'Embracing?' the One-Child Rule: Understanding New Fertility Trends in a Central China Village," *China Quarterly*, no. 192 (December 2007): 855–75. Also see Hong Zhang, "China's New Rural Daughters Coming of Age: Downsizing the Family and Firing Up Cash-Earning Power in the New Economy," *Signs* 32, no. 3 (2007): 671–98.

13. Junhong Chu, "Prenatal Sex Determination and Sex-Selective Abortion in Rural Central China," *Population and Development Review* 27, no. 2 (June 2001): 259–81.

14. Weixing Zhu, Li Lu, and Terese Hesketh, "China's Excess Males, Sex Selective Abortion, and the One Child Policy: Analysis of Data from the 2005 National Intercensus Survey," *British Medical Journal*, April 9, 2009 (BMJ. 2009; 338: b1211).

15. Goodkind, "Child Underreporting, Fertiity, and Sex Ratio Imbalance in China," makes this argument. Among other things, girls, more likely to be born after a son (Ebenstein, "The Missing Girls of China"), are more likely to be hidden as prohibited births than boys born after a daughter.

16. Juhua Yang, "Fertility Squeeze and Gender Bias: A Quantitative and Qualitative Analysis of Birth Planning Policy and Sex Ratio at Birth in China," paper presented at Population Association of America 2012 Annual Meetings, http://paa2012.princeton.edu/papers/120542, finds similar sentiments in interviews (9) although she interprets them somewhat differently, stressing that the policy encourages people to pursue a son while the villagers I spoke to stressed that the policy prevented people from having a daughter. Both seem to be true if one accepts the importance of the two-gender ideal for many people.

17. In another twist on this view, we heard more than once that "two daughters were better than one son."

18. See Yang, "Fertility Squeeze and Gender Bias," figure 5 on 28. Also see Ebenstein, "The Missing Girls of China," in note 21 below.

19. In 2007, 20,000 yuan was often mentioned in a slightly-below-average rural area as the going rate for the first overquota birth.

20. This doctor also arranged adoptions for birth parents that wanted to hide out-of-plan births that occurred in her clinic, claiming the babies were anonymously "abandoned" in the clinic. Doctors and medical personnel in obstetric facilities became increasingly important facilitators for adoptions as outright abandonment declined in the 2000s.

21. Ebenstein, "The Missing Girls of China," 9, presents census data and other evidence that those relatively fewer women who had a second birth after a son sex selected for a daughter; Daniel Goodkind argues that this practice in 1.5-child policy areas contributes to somewhat higher nonregistration for girls than boys because daughters born after a son are overquota while boys born after a girl are not. See Goodkind, "Child Underreporting, Fertiity, and Sex Ratio Imbalance in China." Not surprisingly, a high ranking birth planning official commented that if China moved to a simple two-child policy, there would likely be more use of ultrasound to sex select girls to achieve the one boy and one girl ideal.

This would have the salutary effect of lessening the sex ratio but would increase the illegal practice of sex selective abortion. Wikileaks, Notes from US Embassy in Beijing.

22. Ethan Michelson, "Family Planning Enforcement in Rural China: Enduring State-Society Conflict?," in *Growing Pains: Tensions and Opportunity in China's Transformation*, ed. Jean Oi, Scott Rozelle, and Xueguang Zhou (Stanford, CA: Walter Shorenstein Asia-Pacific Research Center, 2009), chap. 8. Noncompliance with birth planning birth quotas in the countryside was estimated to be about 30 percent of births in the mid-1990s. Although sex selection is a form of noncompliance, it avoids more overt forms of noncompliance such as abandonment and hiding children that raise actual fertility rates. By 2010 many demographers argued that China's fertility rate was close to the policy level; this was born out by the 2011 census, which showed a surprisingly low fertility rate of 1.5. On the decline of fertility desires and greater compliance in rural areas in the 2000s, see Hong Zhang, "From Resisting to 'Embracing?' the One-Child Rule: Understanding New Fertility Trends in a Central China Village."

23. E.g., Wang Feng, "Can China Afford to Continue its One Child Policy?," *Asia Pacific Issues*, East-West Center, No. 77, March 2005, 9. Also see T. White, *China's Longest Campaign*, chap. 9; and Greenhalgh and Winckler, *Governing China's Population*, chaps. 5, 6.

24. In discussions about this issue, some who created families in the 1990s argued that what they dealt with was periodically worse, but it waxed and waned and was more subject to the softening effects of "guanxi" and "corruption." Interviews where we heard these views took place in six different counties (Feixi, Feidong, Changfeng, Fuyang, Funan, Lixin). Significant levels of coercion have cropped up in reports from many other places in the 2000s (including the period since 2005) such as Shandong (the case of Chen Guangcheng, the "blind activist" and lawyer), Guangxi (2007 riots), Guizhou, Zhenyuan (discussed below), Hunan, Shaoyang area (Gaoping, discussed below), Xiamen ("Forced Abortions for Chinese Women," *Al Jazeera*, October 20, 2010), Guangdong ("Old Folks Held to Force Relatives' Sterilizations," *Shanghai Daily*, April 16, 2010, http://www.china.org.cn/china/2010-04/16/content_19831641.htm), Shaanxi (Evan Osnos, "Abortion and Politics in China." *New Yorker*, June 15, 2012).

25. See Liu Xin, "Shandong County Denies 'Abortion Quotas,'" *Global Times*, May 26, 2015, http://www.globaltimes.cn/content/923688.shtml?utm_content

=bufferc5d57&utm_medium=social&utm_source=twitter.com&utm
_campaign=buffer.

26. See, e.g., "Old Folks Held to Force Relatives' Sterilizations," *Shanghai Daily*, April 16, 2010.

27. Shangguan Jiaoming, "In Hunan, Family Planning Turns to Plunder," Caixin Online (English), May 10, 2011, http://english.caing.com/2011–05–10 /100257756.html.

28. This risk seemed to worsen in the 2000s, but perhaps the media first noticed this older pattern in a few areas at this time.

29. A good example of this hybrid form of removing an "illegal" child from its family and village is illustrated by a woman from Changle, Fujian, quoted by John Leland, "For Adoptive Parents, Questions without Answers," *New York Times*, September 18, 2011. Ms. Chen sadly handed her second daughter to an official in exchange for avoiding mandatory sterilization and regaining the right to have another child, hopefully a son, in four years. Zhenyuan (below) has similar cases.

30. Interview, 1996; multiple follow-up interviews with Ding, Huang, and Xiao Yanzi, 1998–2012.

31. Certain identifying details of this account have been changed or omitted to hide identities. The central features of the story remain unchanged.

32. Interview, 1998.

33. At ten years old, a child must give consent to an adoption according to the regulations of this and other orphanages we visited.

34. Documentary films *Daughter's Return* and *Sophia's Journey* directed and produced by Changfu Chang (2011) provide examples of international adoptions in which it is discovered that the children were taken by government officials from Chinese families who were temporarily fostering or had adopted an out-of-plan child who was then placed in an orphanage. In most years domestic adoptions from orphanages exceeded international adoptions, so it is possible that many such children have also been placed domestically, although it may seem safer as well as more lucrative to orphanage officials to place these children internationally so previous parents cannot try to find them.

35. Leslie Wang, Iris Ponte, and Elizabeth Ollen, "Letting Her Go: Western Adoptive Families' Search and Reunion with Chinese Birth Parents," *Adoption Quarterly* 18 (2015): 45–66. A successful birth parent search and reunion, near our research area, is shown in the film *Somewhere Between*, directed by Linda Knowlton (Docuramafilms, 2012).

36. Although the adoptive parents, who found their daughter at their door, did not know who the birth parents were, someone near the village did, leading to tearful reunion and great relief for the birth parents, who had gone to the orphanage in a futile effort to find their daughter after they learned the government had taken her. The orphanage would not tell them anything about their daughter except that she was gone.

37. Interviews, 2008, 2009, 2010, 2011.

38. We learned about this man through a network of international adoptive parents that will not be identified.

39. This is the hidden child case recounted earlier in chapter 3.

40. In other areas and at different times, collecting fines might be the top priority in order to finance the local government. A long interview with a group of five migrants from a village near Kaifeng, Henan, in 2011 revealed how their township officials sold "permission for overquota births" in advance to villagers who were willing to pay in full ahead of time, even before the pregnancy. Sometimes these were offered to people immediately after the birth of a first (boy) or second (girl) child. It was well known, they said, that this was how the government financed itself. They got their money, and local people were not harassed or threatened during their pregnancies. They considered this corrupt, but on the other hand, they had never heard of officials taking away an "illegal" child. Disputes were settled with money. They assumed that officials falsified their birth planning records.

41. Among other things, these laws embody and protect the principle of the "legal clean break" that cancels a child's ties to preadoptive kin and incorporates him or her into the US adoptive family as discussed in Barbara Yngvesson, "Refiguring Kinship in the Space of Adoption," *Anthropological Quarterly* 80, no. 2 (Spring 2007): 561–79. US immigration policy for adopted children from Chinese orphanages requires this "clean break," with official certification that the child has been "irrevocably abandoned" by its biological parents.

42. The 2002 *Population and Family Planning Law of the People's Republic of China* (http://english1.english.gov.cn/laws/2005-10/11/content_75954.htm) states twice that officials may not "infringe on the legitimate rights and interests of citizens" without specifying what these might be, even though the law specifies other prohibited activities in great detail, such as taking bribes, falsifying birth permits, falsifying population statistics, performing abortion for the purposes of sex selection, performing fake birth planning operations, etc. It is not surprising that birth planning abuses of citizens are rarely prosecuted and

fail when they are, sometimes landing the lawyer in jail, as in the case of Chen Guangcheng, the blind activist who took a local class-action suit to court in Shandong in 2005.

43. Two of these parents tried to pursue their case against confiscation in court, but failed.

44. Pang, *Orphans of Shao*, 200.

45. A best-selling, quickly banned investigative report on common abuses in rural Anhui in the early 2000s is Chen Guidi and Wu Chuntao, *Will the Boat Sink the Water? The Life of China's Peasants*, trans. Zhu Hong (New York: PublicAffairs, 2006).

46. "United in grief farmers lament loss of children 'stolen' by officials," *South China Morning Post*, March 21, 2006, 7.

47. The census report, showing an ultra-low total fertility rate below 1.5, an increasingly skewed sex ratio, and a rapidly aging population, sparked renewed calls for the one-child policy to change or end. See Yi Fuxian, "Editorial," *Economic Observer*, May 5, 2011. The Caixin reports were part of that effort.

48. Shangguan Jiaoming, "In Hunan, Family Planning Turns to Plunder," Caixin Online (English), May 10, 2011, http://english.caing.com/2011-05 -10/100257756.html. The story was later picked up by international media; e.g., Sharon LaFraniere, "Chinese Officials Seized and Sold Babies, Parents Say," *New York Times*, August 4, 2011, http://www.nytimes.com/2011/08/05 /world/asia/05kidnapping.html?pagewanted=all.

49. Pang, *Orphans of Shao*.

50. This fee was raised to $5,000 in 2008, partly reflecting the changing exchange rate.

51. "City Says No Babies Seized for Adoption," People's Daily Online, September 30, 2011, http://english.peopledaily.com.cn/90882/7608320.html#.

52. The detailed notes for these stories are in Pang, *The Orphans of Shao*. Some of the shorter published news stories miss or misinterpret the facts of some of these stories. Reporters are also surprisingly unaware of regulations and laws that are used against parents and how they operate, although Pang does a much better job than most others. E.g., the widely publicized case of Yang Libing was reported to involve Yang's "legal birth child" because she was his first child. But the child was illegal and out of plan in numerous ways—forty-two-year-old Yang was not and could not be legally married to his seventeen-year-old underage de facto wife, though they held a traditional banquet at his home. It was later revealed that he was also not the child's biological father, though

this would be of less concern to birth planning regulations than the fact they were not legally married and that the mother was too young to be married and did not have a permitted birth. On the other hand, Yang was later told that he could legally adopt a child because of his age and childless status. He also remained unmarried, in law as well as actuality because his de facto wife left him after her birth daughter was taken.

53. See, e.g., Edward Wong, "Forced to Abort, Chinese Woman under Pressure," *New York Times,* June 26, 2012, http://www.nytimes.com/2012/06/27/world/asia/chinese-family-in-forced-abortion-case-still-under-pressure.html?_r=0.

54. The Chinese government is not alone in asserting that legally sanctioned adoption procedures cannot be considered "selling" or "trafficking" even if large sums of money are involved, as long as these operate under an officially regulated and approved system. Legally regulated private domestic adoptions in the United States also may involve large amounts of money paid out by adopters to lawyers, agencies, and sometimes birth mothers. Adoption has spawned a network of legal ostensibly regulated businesses, providing jobs and incomes to vast numbers of people. Outside of government-sanctioned channels, these same jobs and activities may be seen as child trafficking.

55. Quoted from a Hunan web-based news portal by Sharon LaFraniere, "China Fires 12 after Inquiry on Adoptions," *New York Times,* September 30, 2011, A6.

56. "City Says No Babies Seized for Adoption," People's Daily Online, September 30, 2011, http://english.peopledaily.com.cn/90882/7608320.html#.

57. LaFraniere, "Chinese Officials Seized and Sold Babies."

58. Bao Xiaodong, "'Manufacturing' Abandoned Infants," *Southern Metropolitan News,* July 1, 2009; http://gcontent.oeeee.com/d/fb/dfb84a11f431c624/Blog/c79/662656.html, English translation available at Research-China. Yang Jibin, "Foundling X—May Finally Be Seen Clearly," Big Window Internet Diary, June 16, 2009, http://hi.baidu.com/%C2%B7%BC%FB%B2%BB%C6%BD%C3%BB%D3%D0%B5%B6/blog/item/05dbec6289fde7d4e7113a8e.html (no longer online).

59. Steven Mosher, "'Illegal' Babies Abducted by Chinese Population Control Officials," *Population Research Institute,* Weekly Briefing, 13 (2011), http://www.pop.org/content/illegal-babies-abducted-chinese-population-control-officials.

60. Gu Baochang et al., "China's Local and National Fertility Policies at the End of the Twentieth Century," *Population and Development Review* 33, no. 1 March 2007): 129–47, 140.

61. Australian Government, Migration Review Tribunal, Refugee Review Tribunal, *Background Paper China: Family Planning*, March 8, 2013, 11–15, http://www.refworld.org/pdfid/51f61ea04.pdf.

62. See note 40 above and the vague language pertaining to rights in the *Population and Family Planning Law of the People's Republic of China* implemented in 2002.

63. Bao, "'Manufacturing' Abandoned Infants."

64. Pang, *Orphans of Shao*, 96–99.

65. In interviews, parents whose children were taken from them by government officials considered this kidnapping and likened government fines to a kind of ransom. "United in Grief Farmers Lament Loss of Children 'Stolen' by Officials," *South China Morning Post*, March 21, 2006, 7.

66. Edward Wong, "Population Control Is Called Big Revenue Source in China," *New York Times*, September 26, 2013, http://www.nytimes.com/2013/09/27/world/asia/chinese-provinces-collected-billions-in-family-planning-fines-lawyer-says.html?_r=0.

67. Tyrene White, personal communication.

68. In December 2014, local media in Linyi, Shandong, reported that a ten-month-old baby was taken from parents to force them to pay an exorbitant fine and likely submit to sterilization. The pattern was a familiar one: Linyi, with many recorded birth planning abuses over the years, was under great pressure to correct its poor birth planning record in 2014. Liu Xin, "Shandong County Denies 'Abortion Quotas.'"

69. Wei Yingjie, "China's One-Child Policy Leads to a Racket of Fines, Kidnapping, Foreign Adoptions," *Economic Observer*, October 3, 2011, http://www.worldcrunch.com/culture-society/china-s-one-child-policy-leads-to-racket-of-fines-kidnapping-foreign-adoptions-/c3s3864/#.UxzUahbA5UQ.

CHAPTER FIVE

1. Domestic adoptions from orphanages usually brought in lower fees through most of this period, although by 2009 we found the fees charged Chinese and international adopters were similar in the places we visited.

2. Kay Johnson, "Politics of International and Domestic adoption in China," *Law and Society Review* 36, no. 2 (2002): 379–96.

3. Deng Fei, "The Hengyang Infant Dealing Case: Benevolence or Vice," *Fenghuang Weekly*, February 2, 2006; English translation on Research-China.org,

October 9, 2006. Similarly in the early 1990s, Wuhan officials believed, rightly or wrongly, that babies left in the countryside were likely to die before being picked up. Interviews 1991, 1993.

4. Interview 1998.

5. Scott Tong, "The Dark Side of Adoptions," *Market Place*, May 5, 2010; "Interviewing the Duan Family Matriarch," August 10, 2010, blog post on The Rest of the Story, Research-China.org.

6. In 1996 we also interviewed a garbage recycler who had found almost a dozen babies and had several brought to him and his wife by others. They did not know of any local orphanage that would take these babies, but quickly found local adopters for the healthy ones. They kept and raised those with disabilities, four in total; two infants that they found had died.

7. Scott Tong, "The Dark Side of Adoptions"; "Interviewing the Duan Family Matriarch."

8. A vice director of an orphanage told us in 2010 that they would not even reimburse the cost of the taxi to a finder who brought a baby to their orphanage, for fear of being accused of "buying babies." He claimed they had not paid finder's fees in past either but the Hunan case was well known to directors. This particular orphanage received fewer than four or five healthy babies a year after around 2007. In 2010 when we interviewed him, they had none. Whatever healthy children they received were adopted to local adopters.

9. Chen Zhijin quoted in "Interviewing the Duan Family Matriarch." Scott Tong, "The Dark Side of Adoptions"; Barbara Demick, "Some Chinese Parents Say Their Children Were Stolen for Adoption."

10. Ni Dandan, "Chinese Parents Compete with Foreign Applicants to Adopt Healthy Babies," *Global Times*, April 2, 2014, http://www.globaltimes.cn /content/852341.shtml#.Uz2kgxbA5UQ.

11. Gu Baochang et al., "China's Local and National Fertility Policies at the End of the Twentieth Century," *Population and Development Review* 33, no. 1 (March 2007): 129–47. According to Gu et al., Jiangxi, Sichuan, and Chongqing also had fertility rates that exceeded "policy fertility" by more than other areas.

12. Beech, "China's Baby Traffickers," http://www.time.com/time/asia/magazine /2001/0108/babies.smuggle.html.

13. Wang Li, an illegal middleman, quoted in the documentary film *China's Stolen Children*, directed by Kate Blewett and Brian Woods (2007).

14. The documentary *China's Stolen Children* (2008) provides a glimpse at the

problem of kidnapping as well as the emergence of facilitators whose business involved connecting potential adopters and birth parents, linking both practices to China's birth planning regime.

15. *China's Stolen Children* interviews many parents and investigators who are highly critical of the police's inadequate response to reports of kidnapping. Also see Charles Custer and Leia Li's film *Living with Dead Hearts* (2013).

16. Li Qian, "Adoption Website Raid Saves 382 Babies," *Shanghai Daily*, March 1, 2014, http://www.shanghaidaily.com/national/Adoption-website-raids-save -382-babies/shdaily.shtml.

17. See, e.g., ibid.

18. Yang Xin, "Latest Trafficking Scandal a Wake Up Call for Adoption Reform," *Beijing Today*, January 30, 2015, http://beijingtoday.com.cn/2015/01/latest -trafficking-scandal-wake-call-adoption-reform/.

19. Louise Watt, "China Rescues 89 Children as Young as 10 Days, Arrests 369 Suspects," AP, July 27, 2011, http://news.yahoo.com/china-rescues-89-trafficked -children-arrests-369-044433173.html.

20. Ibid.; Li Qian, "Adoption Website Raid Saves 382 Babies."

21. Chen Shiqu, head of the human trafficking task force of the Public Security ministry, explicitly equated "selling" with "kidnapping" in an interview on National Public Radio: "Selling babies online is in reality kidnapping and selling for money." Didi Kirsten Tatlow, "Crackdown on Baby Trafficking Zeros in on Websites," *New York Times* blog, February 28, 2014.

22. "Public Security Bureau Will Carry Out a Concentrated Search for Thirteen Categories of Children with Unknown Origins," Xinhuanet (Chinese), August 3, 2011, http://www.qianhuaweb.com/content/2011-08/03/content _1934577.htm.

23. Charles T. Lee, "Bare Life, Interstices, and the Third Space of Citizenship," *Women's Studies Quarterly* 38, nos. 1 and 2 (Spring/Summer 2010): 57–81, 57.

24. "China to Tighten Adoption Measures," *China Daily*, August 16, 2011, http:// www.china.org.cn/china/2011-08/16/content_23217599.htm. Also see "China Bans Private Adoptions of Abandoned Infants," Associated Press, Beijing, June 18, 2013, http://bigstory.ap.org/article/china-bans-private -adoptions-abandoned-infants.

25. "China to Tighten Adoption Measures."

26. In practice few children can fit this category, although it exists in the adoption law. The child of a prisoner without relatives, the child of utterly destitute parents without close relatives, etc., might qualify, but we had none in our sample.

27. Guan Xiaofeng, "China Eases Restrictions on Illegally Adopted Children," *China Daily*, September 24, 2008, http://www.chinadaily.com.cn/china /2008-09/24/content_7054640.htm.

28. Yang, "Latest Trafficking Scandal a Wake Up Call for Adoption Reform."

29. Pang, *Orphans of Shao*, 263.

30. Adoption statistics taken from China Civil Affairs Statistical Yearbook for various years. These registered domestic adoption figures compare to international adoption that peaked at fourteen thousand in 2005 and has fallen to below four thousand in 2013. International adoptions, all of which are from orphanages, rose to about 25 percent of total registered adoptions in 2005 but in most years before and since has hovered closer to 12–13 percent of all registered adoptions.

31. Zheng Jinran, "Adoption of Orphans on Downward Trend," *China Daily*, June 18, 2014, http://usa.chinadaily.com.cn/china/2014–06/18/content _17596006.htm.

32. An excellent recent article on this problem is Nathan VanderKlippe, "The Ghost Children: In the Wake of China's One-Child Policy, a Generation Is Lost," *Globe and Mail*, March 13, 2015, http://www.theglobeandmail.com /news/world/the-ghost-children-in-the-wake-of-chinas-one-child-policy-a -generation-is-lost/article23454402/.

33. Interviews (2011–12) with recent adopters from state orphanages in our research area. Orphanage fees ranged from 30,000 to 50,000 yuan, the same or higher than international adoption fees. In 2011 an orphanage in a small city received a 100,000 yuan "donation" from a particularly wealthy domestic adopter in what seemed to be a kind of competition for the handful of healthy children available in the orphanage.

CHAPTER SIX

1. "China Baby Trafficking: 1,094 Suspects Arrested," *Sky News*, February 28, 2014, http://news.sky.com/story/1218781/china-baby-trafficking-1094-suspects -arrested.

2. http://www.usatoday.com/story/opinion/2014/01/18/march-life-abortion -roe-wade-column/4523723/.

3. Aside from numerous cases we found, this is also portrayed in one of the cases in Changfu Chang's documentary *Daughters' Return* (2011).

4. Ni Dandan, "Chinese Parents Compete with Foreign Applicants to Adopt Healthy Babies."

5. Children adopted from orphanages in China must be certified as "irrevocably

abandoned" or a true orphan with both parents dead. Orphanages and Civil Affairs routinely certify children available for international adoption as "abandoned" through a process agreed upon by the United States as sufficient for its purposes.

6. Yngvesson, *Belonging in an Adopted World*.

7. The use of the term "bare life" here is to draw parallels with the classic understanding of this concept by Georgio Agamben, *Homo Sacer: Sovereign Power and Bare Life* (Stanford, CA: Stanford University Press, 1998). Although the usefulness of this concept has not been explored here, it deserves further study and elaboration in this context.

8. Liu Jihong et al., "Physical Well-Being and School Enrollment," cited in chapter 3.

9. Greenhalgh, *Cultivating Global Citizens*.

10. Kay Johnson, "China's One Child Policy: Not Yet in the Dustbin of History," *DifferenTakes*, no. 83, Winter 2014.

11. In addition to the cases shown here, see VanderKlippe, "Ghost Children," for recent urban cases. He also interviews a twenty-one-year-old, a second daughter born in Beijing, who has fought her entire life to gain the right to a legal existence.

12. Susan Greenhalgh, "Planned Births, Unplanned Persons," *American Ethnologist* 30, no. 2 (May 2003).

BIBLIOGRAPHY

Agamben, Georgio. *Homo Sacer: Sovereign Power and Bare Life*. Stanford, CA: Stanford University Press, 1998.

Australian Government, Migration Review Tribunal, Refugee Review Tribunal. *Background Paper China: Family Planning*, March 8, 2013, 11–15. http://www.refworld.org/pdfid/51f61ea04.pdf.

Bao Xiaodong. "'Manufacturing' Abandoned Infants." Southern Metropolitan News (Chinese), July 1, 2009. http://gcontent.oeeee.com/d/fb/dfb84a11f431c624/Blog/c79/662656.html. English translation available at Research-China.org.

Bartholet, Elizabeth. *Family Bonds: Adoption and the Politics of Parenting*. New York: Mariner Books, 1994.

Beech, Hannah. "China's Baby Traffickers." *Time*, January 8, 2001. http://www.time.com/time/asia/magazine/2001/0108/babies.smuggle.html.

Blewett, Kate, and Brian Woods. *China's Stolen Children*. DVD. Directed by Jezza Neumann. HBO, 2008.

———. *The Dying Rooms*. Directed by Brian Wood and Kate Blewett. Lauderdale Productions, 1995.

Bossen, Laurel. "Forty Million Missing Girls." ZNet, October 7, 2005. http://www.zcommunications.org/forty-million-missing-girls-by-laurel-bossen.

Briggs, Laura. "Making 'American' Families: Transnational Adoption and US Latin America Policy." In *Haunted by Empire*, ed. Ann Stoler, 344–65. Durham, NC: Duke University Press, 2006.

———. *Somebody's Children: The Politics of Transracial Adoption.* Durham, NC: Duke University Press, 2012.

Chen Guidi and Wu Chuntao. *Will the Boat Sink the Water? The Life of China's Peasants,* trans. Zhu Hong. New York: PublicAffairs, 2006.

Chang, Changfu. *Daughters' Return: Searching for Birth Parents* (Series 2). DVD. Directed by Changfu Chang. Millersville, PA, 2011.

———. *Ricki's Promise.* DVD. Directed by Changfu Chang. Millersville, PA, 2014.

———. *Sophia's Journey: Searching for Birth Parents* (Series 1). DVD. Directed by Changfu Chang. Millersville, PA, 2011.

"China Baby Trafficking: 1,094 Suspects Arrested." *Sky News,* February 28, 2014. http://news.sky.com/story/1218781/china-baby-trafficking-1094-suspects -arrested.

"China Bans Private Adoptions of Abandoned Infants." Associated Press, Beijing, June 18, 2013. http://bigstory.ap.org/article/china-bans-private-adoptions -abandoned-infants.

"China Child Fines 'Spark Riot.'" BBC News, May 21, 2007. http://news.bbc.co .uk/2/hi/asia-pacific/6677273.stm.

China Civil Affairs Statistical Yearbook. Beijing: Zhongguo Minzheng tongji nian- jian, 1999–2012.

"China to Tighten Adoption Measures." *China Daily,* August 16, 2011. http:// www.china.org.cn/china/2011–08/16/content_23217599.htm.

Chiu, Vivien. "From China with Love." *South China Morning Post,* August 15, 1999.

Christie, Grazi Poso. "Choose Adoption, Not Abortion." *USA Today,* Janu- ary 14, 2014. http://www.usatoday.com/story/opinion/2014/01/18/march -life-abortion-roe-wade-column/4523723/.

Chu, Junhong. "Prenatal Sex Determination and Sex-Selective Abortion in Rural Central China." *Population and Development Review* 27, no. 2 (June 2001): 259–81. doi:10.1111/j.1728–4457.2001.00259.x.

"City Says No Babies Seized for Adoption." *People's Daily Online,* September 30, 2011. http://english.peopledaily.com.cn/90882/7608320.html#.

Convention on the Protection of Children and Co-operation in Respect of Inter- country Adoption. May 29, 1993. Hague Conference on Private International Law. www.hcch.net/upload/conventions/txt33en.pdf.

"Court Convicts 52 of Baby-Trafficking in China." *New York Times,* July 7, 2004. http://www.nytimes.com/2004/07/24/world/court-convicts-52-of-baby -trafficking-in-china.html.

Custer, Charles, and Leia Li. *Living with Dead Hearts*. Produced and directed by Charles Custer and Leia Li. ChinaGeeks Films, 2013.

Demick, Barbara. "Some Chinese Parents Say Their Children Were Stolen for Adoption." *Los Angeles Times*, September 20, 2009. http://articles.latimes.com/2009/sep/20/world/fg-china-adopt20.

Deng Fei. "The Hengyang Infant Dealing Case: Benevolence or Vice." *Fenghuang Weekly*, February 2, 2006. English translation on Research-China.org, October 9, 2006.

Dorow, Sara, and Amy Swiffen. "Blood and Desire: The Secret of Heteronormativity in Adoption Narratives of Culture." *American Ethnologist* 36, no. 3 (August 2009): 563–73.

Dryzek, John. *Politics of the Earth: Environmental Discourses*. Oxford: Oxford University Press, 2005.

Ebenstein, Avraham. "The Missing Girls of China and the Unintended Consequences of the One Child Policy." *Journal of Human Resources* 45, no. 1 (Winter 2010).

Evans, Karin. *The Lost Daughters of China*. New York: Tarcher, 2000.

Fong, Vanessa. *Only Hope: Coming of Age under China's One Child Policy*. Palo Alto, CA: Stanford University Press, 2004.

"Forced Abortions for Chinese Women." Al Jazeera, October 20, 2010. http://www.aljazeera.com/news/asia-pacific/2010/10/201010208145793266.html.

"Forced Abortion of Pregnant Shaanxi Women Who Failed to Pay 40,000 Birth Planning Fine." *64 Tianwang*, June 11, 2012 (Chinese). http://www.64tianwang.com/bencandy.php?fid-7-id-10243-page-1.htm.

"Found 'Black Child' Still Has Not Obtained a Hukou." *Hefei Wanbao*, February 2, 2010.

Goodkind, Daniel. "Child Underreporting, Fertility, and Sex Ratio Imbalance in China." *Demography* 48 (2011): 291–316. doi:10.1007/s13524-010-0007-y.

Goodman, Ellen. "Cloe's First Fourth." *Boston Globe*, July 3, 2003, A13.

Goodman, Paul. "Stealing Babies for Adoption." *Washington Post*, March 12, 2006, A01.

Graff, E. J. "The Lie We Love." *Foreign Policy*, November 1, 2008.

Greenhalgh, Susan. *Cultivating Global Citizens: Population in the Rise of China*. Cambridge, MA: Harvard University Press, 2010.

———. *Just One Child: Science and Policy in Deng's China*. Berkeley: University of California Press, 2008.

———. "Patriarchal Demographics? China's Sex Ratio Reconsidered." *Population and Development Review* 38, supplement (2012): 130–49.

———. "Planned Births, Unplanned Persons." *American Ethnologist* 30, no. 2 (May 2003).

Greenhalgh, Susan, Zhu Chuzhu, and Li Nan. "Restraining Population Growth in Three Chinese Villages, 1988–1993." *Population and Development Review* 20, no.2 (1994): 365–95.

Greenhalgh, Susan, and Edwin Winckler. *Governing China's Population.* Stanford, CA: Stanford University Press, 2005.

Gu, Baochang, et. al. "China's Local and National Fertility Policies at the End of the Twentieth Century." *Population and Development Review* 33, no. 1 (March 2007): 129–47.

Guan Xiaofeng. "China Eases Restrictions on Illegally Adopted Children." *China Daily*, September 24, 2008. http://www.chinadaily.com.cn/china/2008-09/24/content_7054640.htm.

Guterl, Mathew. *Seeing Race in Modern America.* Chapel Hill: University of North Carolina, 2013.

Hartmann, Betsy. "The Great Distraction: 'Overpopulation' Is Back in Town." *Common Dreams*, August 30, 2011. https://www.commondreams.org/view/2011/08/30-1.

Hopgood, Mei-ling. *Lucky Girl: A Memoir.* Chapel Hill, NC: Alonquin Books, 2009.

Hudson, Valerie M., and Andrea M. den Boer. *Bare Branches: The Security Implications of Asia's Excess Male Population.* Cambridge, MA: MIT Press, 2004.

Hvinstendahl, Mara. "Has China Outgrown the One Child Policy?" *Science* 329, no. 5998 (September 2010): 1458–61. doi:10.1126/science.329.5998.1458.

———. *Unnatural Selection: Choosing Boys over Girls, and the Consequences of a World Full of Men.* New York: Public Affairs, 2011.

Jacobson, Heather. *Culture Keeping: White Mothers, International Adoption, and the Negotiation of Family Difference.* Nashville, TN: Vanderbilt University Press, 2008.

Johansson, Sten, and Ola Nygren. "The Missing Girls of China: A New Demographic Account." *Population and Development Review* 17, no. 1 (1991): 35–51.

Johnson, Kay. "Adoption in China." In *Encyclopedia of Modern China.* New York: Charles Scribner's Sons, 2009.

———. "Challenging the Discourse of Intercountry Adoption: Perspectives from

Rural China." In *Intercountry Adoption,* ed. Judith Gibbons and Karen Rotabi, 103–17. Burlington, VT: Ashgate, 2012.

———. "China's One Child Policy: Not Yet in the Dustbin of History." *Differen-Takes,* no. 83, Winter 2014.

———. "Politics of International and Domestic Adoption in China." *Law and Society Review* 36, no. 2 (2002): 379–96.

———. "Saving China's Abandoned Girls." *Australian Journal of Chinese Affairs,* no. 30 (July 1993): 67–84.

———. "Sorrow of the Orphans." *Boston Globe Sunday Globe, Focus,* February 11, 1996.

Johnson, Kay Ann. *Wanting a Daughter, Needing a Son: Abandonment, Adoption, and Orphanage Care in China.* Edited by Amy Klatzkin. Minneapolis: Yeong and Yeong, 2004.

Kasmin, Amy, Patti Waldmeir, and Kirija Shuvakumar. "Asia: Heirs and Spares." *Financial Times,* July 10, 2011. http://www.ft.com/intl/cms/s/0/54751678-ab1a-11e0-b4d8-00144feabdc0.html#axzz1V1igqs22.

Knowlton, Linda Goldstein. *Somewhere Between.* DVD. Docuramafilms, 2012.

LaFraniere, Sharon. "China Fires 12 after Inquiry on Adoptions." *New York Times,* September 30 2011, A6.

———. "Chinese Officials Seized and Sold Babies, Parents Say." *New York Times,* August 4, 2011. http://www.nytimes.com/2011/08/05/world/asia/05kidnapping.html?pagewanted=all.

Lee, Charles T. "Bare Life, Interstices, and the Third Space of Citizenship." *Women's Studies Quarterly* 38, nos. 1 and 2 (Spring/Summer 2010): 57–81.

Lee, James, and Wang Feng. *One-Quarter of Humanity: Malthusian Mythology and Chinese Reality.* Cambridge, MA: Harvard University Press, 1999.

Leland, John. "For Adoptive Parents, Questions without Answers." *New York Times,* September 16, 2011. http://www.nytimes.com/2011/09/18/nyregion/chinas-adoption-scandal-sends-chills-through-families-in-united-states.html?pagewanted=all&_r=0.

Li Qian. "Adoption Website Raid Saves 382 Babies." *Shanghai Daily,* March 1, 2014. http://www.shanghaidaily.com/national/Adoption-website-raids-save-382-babies/shdaily.shtml.

Li, Shuzhuo, Yexia Zhang, and Marcus Feldman. "Birth Registration in China: Problems, Practices, and Policies." *Population Research and Policy Review* 29 (2010): 297–317. doi:10.1007/s11113-009-9141-x.

Liao, Huijian. "Child Brides Resurface in China with Shortage of Females." *Want*

China Times, May 30, 2011. http://www.wantchinatimes.com/news-subclass -cnt.aspx?cid=1503&MainCatID=&id=20110530000003.

Liu, Jihong, et al. "Factors Affecting Adoption in China, 1950–1980." *Population Studies* 58, no. 1 (March 2004): 21–36.

Liu, Jihong, Grace Wyshak, and Ulla Larsen. "Physical Well-Being and School Enrolment: A Comparison of Adopted and Biological Children in One-Child Families." *Social Science & Medicine* 59 (2004): 609–23. doi:10.1016/j. socscimed.2003.11.008.

Liu Xin. "Shandong County Denies 'Abortion Quotas.'" *Global Times*, May 26, 2015. http://www.globaltimes.cn/content/923688.shtml?utm_content =bufferc5d57&utm_medium=social&utm_source=twitter.com&utm _campaign=buffer.

Louis, Elaine. "Now Chosen, Chinese Girls Take to the US." *New York Times*, April 27, 1995.

Marovich, Maureen. *Invisible Red Thread*. DVD. Directed by Changfu Chang and Maureen Marovich. Picture This Productions, 2011.

Michelson, Ethan. "Family Planning Enforcement in Rural China: Enduring State-Society Conflict?" In *Growing Pains: Tensions and Opportunity in China's Transformation*, ed. Jean Oi, Scott Rozelle, and Xueguang Zhou, chap. 8. Stanford, CA: Walter Shorenstein Asia-Pacific Research Center, 2009.

Mosher, Steven. "'Illegal' Babies Abducted by Chinese Population Control Officials." *Population Research Institute*, Weekly Briefing, 13 (2011). http:// www.pop.org/content/illegal-babies-abducted-chinese-population-control -officials.

Munroe, Robin, and Jeff Rigsby. *Death by Default: A Policy of Fatal Neglect in China's State Orphanages*. New York: Human Rights Watch, 1996.

Ni Dandan. "Chinese Parents Compete with Foreign Applicants to Adopt Healthy Babies." *Global Times*, April 2, 2014. http://www.globaltimes.cn/content /852341.shtml#.Uz2kgxbA5UQ

"Old Folks Held to Force Relatives' Sterilizations." *Shanghai Daily*, April 16, 2010. http://www.china.org.cn/china/2010–04/16/content_19831641.htm.

Osnos, Evan. "Abortion and Politics in China." *New Yorker*, June 15, 2012. http:// www.newyorker.com/news/letter-from-china/abortion-and-politics-in -china.

Pang Jiaoming. *The Orphans of Shao: A True Account of the Blood and Tears of the One-child Policy in China*. New York: Women's Rights in China Publishers, 2014. English version.

Park, Nicholas, and Patricia Hill. "Is Adoption an Option?" *Journal of Family Issues* 35, no. 5 (April 2014): 601–26. http://jfi.sagepub.com/content/35/5/601.

Population and Family Planning Law of the People's Republic of China (Order of the President No. 63). December, 29, 2001; implemented September 1, 2002.

Porter, Bruce. "I Met My Daughter at the Wuhan Foundling Hospital—Unwanted and Abandoned, Baby Girls Have Become the Newest Chinese Export." *New York Times Magazine*, April, 11, 1993.

"Public Security Bureau Will Carry Out a Concentrated Search for Thirteen Categories of Children with Unknown Origins." *Xinhuanet* (Chinese), August 3, 2011. http://www.qianhuaweb.com/content/2011-08/03/content_1934577 .htm.

Research-China.org. "Interviewing the Duan Family Matriarch." August 10, 2010, The Rest of the Story. http://research-china-trs3.blogspot.com/?zx= a17c84a8700bded3.

Riley, Nancy, and Krista Van Vleet. *Making Families through Adoption*. Los Angeles: Sage, 2012.

Selman, Peter. "The Global Decline in International Adoption: What Lies Ahead?" *Social Policy and Society* 11, no. 3 (July 2012): 381–97. doi:http://dx.doi.org/10 .1017/S1474746412000085.

Shangguan Jiaoming. "In Hunan, Family Planning Turns to Plunder." Caixin Online (English), May 10, 2011. http://english.caing.com/2011–05–10 /100257756.html.

Tatlow, Didi Kirsten. "Crackdown on Baby Trafficking Zeros in on Websites." *New York Times* blog, February 28, 2014. http://sinosphere.blogs.nytimes.com /2014/02/28/crackdown-on-baby-trafficking-zeros-in-on-websites/.

Tong, Scott. "The Dark Side of Adoptions." *MarketPlace*, May 5, 2010. http://www .marketplace.org/topics/life/dark-side-chinese-adoptions.

"United in Grief Farmers Lament Loss of Children 'Stolen' by Officials." *South China Morning Post*, March 21, 2006, 7. http://www.scmp.com/article /541264/united-grief-farmers-lament-loss-children-stolen-officials.

VanderKlippe, Nathan. "The Ghost Children: In the Wake of China's One-Child Policy, a Generation Is Lost," *Globe and Mail*, March 13, 2015. http:// www.theglobeandmail.com/news/world/the-ghost-children-in-the-wake-of -chinas-one-child-policy-a-generation-is-lost/article23454402/.

Wang, Feng. "Can China Afford to Continue Its One Child Policy?" Asia Pacific Issues 77, East-West Center, March 2005. http://www.eastwestcenter.org /fileadmin/stored/pdfs/api077.pdf.

———. "China's Population Destiny: The Looming Crisis." Brookings Research, September 2010. http://www.brookings.edu/research/articles/2010/09/china-population-wang.

Wang, Leslie, Iris Ponte, and Elizabeth Ollen. "Letting Her Go: Western Adoptive Families' Search and Reunion with Chinese Birth Parents." *Adoption Quarterly* 18 (2015): 45–66.

Watt, Louise. "China Rescues 89 children as young as 10 days, arrests 369 suspects." AP, July 27, 2011. http://news.yahoo.com/china-rescues-89-trafficked-children-arrests-369-044433173.html.

Wei Yingjie. "China's One-Child Policy Leads to a Racket of Fines, Kidnapping, Foreign Adoptions." *Economic Observer*, October 3, 2011. http://www.worldcrunch.com/culture-society/china-s-one-child-policy-leads-to-racket-of-fines-kidnapping-foreign-adoptions-/c3s3864/#.UxzUahbA5UQ.

"Welfare Institutes' Income Paid by Foreign Adoption Donations Questioned." *Beijing News*, June 9, 2011. http://blog.sina.com.cn/s/blog_4ab34fd101017ko3.htm (Chinese).

White, Tyrene. *China's Longest Campaign: Birth Planning in the People's Republic, 1949–2005.* Ithaca, NY: Cornell University Press, 2006.

———. "Domination, Resistance, and Accommodation in China's One-Child Campaign." In *Chinese Society: Change, Conflict, and Resistance,* ed. Elizabeth Perry and Mark Selden, 171–96. 3rd ed. New York: Routledge, 2010.

Whyte, Martin King, Wang Feng, and Yong Cai. "Challenging Myths about China's One-Child Policy." *China Journal,* no. 74 (July 2015), 144–59.

Wikileaks. Notes from US Embassy in Beijing, 2010.

Wolf, Arthur. "Adopt a Daughter-in-Law, Marry a Sister: A Chinese Solution to the Problem of the Incest Taboo." *American Anthropologist* 70 (1968): 866–74.

Wong, Edward. "Forced to Abort, Chinese Woman under Pressure." *New York Times,* June 26, 2012. http://www.nytimes.com/2012/06/27/world/asia/chinese-family-in-forced-abortion-case-still-under-pressure.html?_r=0.

———. "Population Control Is Called Big Revenue Source in China." *New York Times,* September 26, 2013. http://www.nytimes.com/2013/09/27/world/asia/chinese-provinces-collected-billions-in-family-planning-fines-lawyer-says.html?_r=0.

Xinran. *Message from an Unknown Chinese Mother: Stories of Loss and Love.* New York: Scribner, 2010.

Yan, Yunxiang. "Girl Power: Young Women and the Waning of Patriarchy in

North China." *Ethnology* 45, no. 2 (Spring 2006): 105–23. http://www.jstor
.org/stable/4617569.

Yang Jibin. "Foundling X—May Finally Be Seen Clearly." Big Window Internet Diary, June 16, 2009 (Chinese). http://hi.baidu.com/%C2%B7
%BC%FB%B2%BB%C6%BD%C3%BB%D3%D0%B5%B6/blog/item
/05dbec6289fde7d4e7113a8e.html.

Yang, Juhua. "Fertility Squeeze and Gender Bias: A Quantitative and Qualitative
Analysis of Birth Planning Policy and Sex Ratio at Birth in China." Paper presented at Population Association of America 2012 Annual Meetings, http://
paa2012.princeton.edu/papers/120542.

Yang Xin. "Latest Trafficking Scandal a Wake Up Call for Adoption Reform."
Beijing Today, January 30, 2015. http://beijingtoday.com.cn/2015/01/latest
-trafficking-scandal-wake-call-adoption-reform/.

Yi Fuxian. "Editorial: The Population May Be Aging Even Worse Than the Authorities Admit in the Latest 10-Year Census; Why China Urgently Needs
to Change Its Birth Policy." *Economic Observer*, May 5, 2011. http://www
.worldcrunch.com/china-cooking-books-its-census-data/3017.

Yngvesson, Barbara. *Belonging in an Adopted World: Race, Identity, and Transnational Adoption.* Chicago: University of Chicago Press, 2010.

———. "Refiguring Kinship in the Space of Adoption." *Anthropological Quarterly*
80, no. 2 (Spring 2007): 561–79.

Zhang, Hong. "Bracing for an Uncertain Future: A Case Study of New Coping
Strategies of Rural Parents under China's Birth Control Policy." *China Journal*
54 (July 2005): 53–76.

———. "China's New Rural Daughters Coming of Age: Downsizing the Family and Firing Up Cash-Earning Power in the New Economy." *Signs* 32, no. 3
(2007): 671–98.

———. "From Resisting to 'Embracing?' the One-Child Rule: Understanding
New Fertility Trends in a Central China Village." *China Quarterly*, no. 192
(December 2007): 855–75.

Zhang Longxi. *Mighty Opposites: From Dichotomies to Differences in the Comparative Study of China.* Stanford, CA: Stanford University Press, 1998.

Zhang, Weiguo. "Is a Married-Out Daughter Like Spilt Water?" *Modern China* 35,
no. 3 (May 2009): 256–83.

———. "Who Adopts Girls and Why?" *China Journal* 56 (July 2006): 2–19.

Zheng Jinran. "Adoption of Orphans on Downward Trend." *China Daily*, June 18,

2014. http://usa.chinadaily.com.cn/china/2014–06/18/content_17596006
.htm.

Zhu, Weixing, Li Lu, and Terese Hesketh. "China's Excess Males, Sex Selective
Abortion, and the One Child Policy: Analysis of Data from the 2005 National
Intercensus Survey." *British Medical Journal*, April 9, 2009 (BMJ. 2009; 338:
b1211). http://www.ncbi.nlm.nih.gov/pmc/articles/PMC2667570/.

INDEX

CPSIA information can be obtained
at www.ICGtesting.com
Printed in the USA
BVHW030825210819
556411BV00001B/27/P